CONTENTS

KU-320-741

How nature creates greens shoots

Even in nature it is a mystery. No one knows exactly what is the spark, the starting signal for a seed to start germinating and create a new seedling for becoming a green shoot.

Lying dormant, the seed is a passive, inert, isolated part of nature.

To germinate, seeds need water, oxygen for energy, and a temperature that's right for them.

Many live seeds have what botanists call dormancy, stubbornly refusing to germinate even if its environment has sufficient water and warmth.

Most seeds will also go through a period of quiescence where there is no observable active growth.

Some seeds require particular conditions to germinate, such as heat from a fire, soaking in water, or even being passed through an animal's digestion system to weaken the seed's coat and enable germination.

Age is not necessarily a barrier for a seed's potential for growth: the oldest seed germinated into a viable plant is a 1,300-year-old lotus fruit, recovered from a dry lakebed in northeastern China. With proper care, the average useful life of many seeds can be extended.

The size of the seed can belie its true potential, with the tiniest of seeds able to produce new life well beyond its evident size.

The outside appearance of seeds is deceptive, with its hard outer coat protecting it from the world at large, but also hiding its potential. The seed is home to an embryonic, immature plant with all the parts of the adult waiting to grow.

A typical young seedling consists of three main parts: an embryonic root, shoot seed, and seed leaves. Becoming too large for its shell the embryonic plant bursts open, its root tip emerging downwards to anchor the seed in place, and allow the embryo to absorb water and nutrients from the surrounding soil for the shoot to sprout upwards.

Once the seedling starts to photosynthesize, converting energy from sunlight, it is no longer dependent on its original seed's energy reserves.

Big seeds can feed the embryo plant longer as it works its way toward light, so can usually be planted deeper. Available water is also important to the newly emerged root. In summer when the top of the soil dries out quickly, it can help if the seed is planted a little deeper.

Pre-soaking seeds can speed up the germinating process. You can increase the rate of seeds germination by using specially prepared seedbed boxes to allow plants to grow in controlled conditions, before transplanting them into the ground.

A lot can be done to help the seed's potential success rate for germinating; clearing stones, debris, insect eggs and unwanted diseased spores removes potential barriers. You can enhance the soil by levelling to improve drainage, or break it up to allow more air and water in, or feed the seed's environment with appropriate fertilizer to promote growth.

Further thinning in the seedbed - removing weaker seedlings -helps the remaining shoots to grow stronger because they have more access to direct light while available nutirents are focussed on their growth.

Even the humblest of seeds can produce a remarkable green shoot, capable of becoming the mightiest and largest of life forms on the planet.

1. Welcome to the age of disruption: an era of challenges and opportunities

This is a book about the times we live in.

It is a guide to help anyone cope, make the most of, or even thrive in the unfamiliar and difficult economic circumstances we face.

This is an age of disruption: what was previously thought of as safe, reliable or predictable just doesn't seem to be the case any more.

With doom and gloom in the news, harsh realities hitting home with many losing their jobs, fewer obvious opportunities, and a general slowdown of the economy, we all need help and guidance.

Where can you turn to for help? Who has the answers? Where is the rock of certainty you need in your life?

The problem it seems is that nobody knows. No one seems to have an answer.

It's best summed up by an experience of a friend of mine, a leading motivational speaker. He was at a conference of senior BBC executives. Before him was a business finance expert.

This expert revealed Powerpoint upon Powerpoint of graphs, trends and data essentially showing how the next few years are going to be desperate.

The thought occurred to my friend: did this guy predict the current credit crunch? What was he saying two years ago - and what were his slides predicting then?

Uncomfortably, it seems we cannot turn to the so-called 'experts' to predict what is going to happen and assuage the nervous anxiety about our futures. The answer is, they simply don't know.

In this situation, who can you rely on? There's only one person it seems.

And that is you.

In a period of great disruption, the only certainty you have is yourself, your own capabilities, creative thinking and drive – your resourcefulness.

You have a choice of how you respond to this global economic predicament in the best way possible for your own destiny.

The only certainty in these uncertain times is your own resourcefulness; by making the most of it, it will serve as the best strategy to shape your response to any challenge you face.

The Oscar winning film *'Slumdog Millionaire'* features orphans, slaughter, organised crime, poverty, enslavement and police brutality. It has however, been marketed as a 'feelgood movie'.

If this film is labelled 'feelgood' - perhaps in its story of suffering and renewal, and looking on the bright side of tragedy – then this text too is a 'feelgood' book.

This is not intended to be a smug text, written by a know-it all who amazingly has thrived in the economic downturn. Rather, this is a book to get you thinking in a different way: because we live in different times. What was previously the usual, the expected, is now the unusual, the unexpected, where different rules apply. You cannot trust or indeed expect your usual comfort blankets to be there.

In the age of disruption, you need to think differently. You need to boost your disruptive thinking skills, so you can best adapt, respond, survive, or thrive.

You may even come across, what I refer to in Chapter 9, a 'Golden Swan', an unexpected, outstanding opportunity awaiting your discovery – or more likely, you will stumble upon it.

You are in a David v Goliath situation: little you is facing a giant tidal wave of the negative world economic situation.

The year 2009 witnessed a global economic downturn. It was also the bi-centenary of the birth of Charles Darwin and the 150th anniversary of the publication of his theory of evolution. Paraphrased as 'the survival of the fittest' the theory explained the distinction between animals that survive and the rest.

It is not the biggest, toughest, physically strongest, or most athletic that survive. Just think of the dinosaur and its fate compared to many of its puny yet evolutionary successful neighbours.

Rather, it is the flexibility of the life form - how it is best at responding to any new changes in its environment and how it fits into its new circumstances - which is its lifeline for survival.

The ones that succeed and survive are the ones that show their adaptability and ability to change.

In February 2009 the UK national media also focussed on the opening of a new shop. The store was in a small market town, several hours outside of London. It sold a range of household items such as what you would find in any high street across the country. The business was being opened by a group of people who had just been made redundant.

Nothing remarkable in that you might say. So why did it receive extensive, rapt interest and enthusiasm from world-weary media hacks? How did it inspire Chris Evans, the BBC radio DJ to offer his services for free to perform the store's formal opening when it began trading?

The story was about the opening of a new shop 'Wellworths'. It was one of over 800 Woolworths stores which had been closed when the chain went into administration in late 2008, after almost a century on the high street.

The story was about how Claire Robertson, who was with Woolworths for 18 years and had started with the chain as a Saturday girl, believed her branch in Dorchester, Dorset, could be a viable business.

Except for a change in the name, Wellworths - not Woolworths (which was soon shortened in the news stories to 'Wellies'), there would be very few changes. It still offered pick 'n' mix sweets, home and kitchen items, seasonal products, toys and textiles, along with the same familiar, friendly service. And the store would re-open eventually re-employing 22 staff who had lost their jobs when Woolworths went bust.

Why did such a seemingly mundane story inspire such great interest?

The heart of its appeal is how it represented a positive, shining light, in the dark gloom of negative stories. More importantly, it provided an example of people fighting back, doing something about their fate, standing up to the tide of bad news, bad times and bad prospects.

The Wellworths story captivated the UK audience. It triggered some relief that someone was out there was doing something positive.

Yet what would you do if your personal equivalent of Woolworths was to close? How would you respond to such havoc and negative consequences in your life?

I believe there's a Wellworths story in each of us. Claire Robertson, the Wellworths manager, is not so different from you and I.

At a time when changes are being thrust upon us we need to think and act differently in the age of disruption.

This book aims to provide a valuable resource which boosts your resourcefulness by enhancing your flexible and creative thinking, giving you more tools, power and confidence to create the best response to your circumstances.

It aims to help you maximise your response to the world around you. It is not about how you can survive, but how you can flourish and become a green shoot in the Upturn.

And that's not just economic fulfilment, but choosing and creating the most fulfilling options for you.

Maybe there is a need for a new academic subject to sit alongside economics, sociology and psychology. A discipline based on how we manage personal resourcefulness in response to the world we live in.

We could even call it 'Me-conomics'. This subject could give you pointers about what you can do to make the most of your resources, your ability to flexibly respond to new, unfamiliar and different circumstances.

But in your challenge to be a green shoot, is it all about 'Me'?

I was once at a children's party watching youngsters playing the game Musical Chairs, where the group has to run around a line of alternate facing chairs. When the music stops they each have to sit down. The drama and fun increases each time a chair is removed, with one fewer chair for each child's bottom.

When I was a kid I used to enjoy the game, and now feel the game serves as a useful metaphor for competition around scarce resources.

While watching the youngsters gamely trying to avoid being the one excluded at each round, the winning gameplan for Musical Chairs came to me (admittedly twenty five years too late!)

The secret for getting to the final two in the game is to go really slow. That way you create a space between you and the person in front. By doing so you can easily find a chair, but create congestion for others who struggle and compete for the remaining scarce chairs.

When you are down to the final two children - where you have to run around the last remaining chair and a further object - you have to introduce another tactic to your game plan. Here, you need to use a combination of going dead slow when you are approaching the chair and extremely fast when your opponent is nearer to the chair.

The space in musical chairs is equivalent to creating the space and time around you in your challenge to think flexibly and identify your green shoot in the Upturn. The variation in speed is like your thinking flexibly faster.

If this were a book about 'How to win at Musical Chairs' it could be used to enable you to create different strategies for you to be a winner.

Being successful in the Upturn is just like this; the flexibility of your approach using a combination of different strategies to adjust to varying circumstances will help you succeed.

But this implies a selfish win-lose strategy of 'If there are fewer chairs around I am going to be the person to get one.'

Alternatively, you can used this book to adopt a win-win strategy, taking a view that collectively we will all win in some way, and have a seat, so to speak.

We might then start redefining what we mean by 'sitting'

or 'time on chair' and explore ideas as varied as many people sitting on each other's laps or timesharing the chair.

More radically, we might use this book to redefine the whole situation, using win-win-win thinking and say 'it's a silly game this, let's do something better with our lives to make the world a better place.'

The spine of this book is how you are a green shoot, an agent for change in the wider world. The green shoots of recovery will be the result of a mass of individuals creating their seeds of opportunity.

We live in a world where we build a culture of false prophets, where pessimism decrees that we must knock anyone down who claims they can see green shoots of recovery – particularly when they fail to wish away our personal difficulties in the global economic downturn.

As the fictional character Kilgore Trout created by novelist Kurt Vonnegut, observed in his Kilgore's creed: *"You were sick, but now you're well again, and there's work to do."*

It seems to be a good way to describe our situation: the world has been sick, you're well, and there's work and opportunities to take advantage of.

You have the choice to decide what you need to do. The Romans had a phrase, *'Carpe Diem'* – seize the day. Let's adopt a more contemporary variation of the Latin phrase, *'Carpe Disruption'* – seize the disruption.

2. Sensational times

The Challenge: *There's a lot of bad news out there*

The Opportunity: *There's good news as well*

The Chinese had a proverb 'May you live in interesting times'. It was obviously meant with some ironic understatement.

If I were looking for a phrase to describe our current situation, I wouldn't say we lived in 'interesting times'.

The word I use goes beyond 'interesting'.

We actually live in 'sensational times'.

If you check out the dictionary the word 'sensational' has a number of meanings.

It is often used to describe things which are outstanding and feature a strong emotional dimension. 'Sensational' is therefore an appropriate term to mark the significance and impact of our credit crunch times – and both the bad and good news within it.

Our sensational times: the bad news

The world economy has entered a recession breathtaking for both its speed, and synchronization.

In the 20th century during the Great Depression the UK economy shrunk by 5.5 per cent between 1929 and 1933. During 2008-9 the UK economy shrunk by 4 per cent in just 12 months.

For those hoping for a quick Upturn out of the current banking crisis the precedents are not good. The Swedes took three years to get out of their banking crisis in the early 1990s, their GDP dropping by 6 per cent between 1990 and 1993 and unemployment rising from 3 per cent to 12 per cent

In Japan the Nikkei stock index peaked in 1989 but a year later, had dropped a staggering 43 per cent. As Japan entered the 1990's, a crisis began to emerge in its financial system, a crisis that took an entire decade to play out. (You have to also recognise that for long periods during the Japanese bank crisis there was a boom in world trade.)

It's not good news either if you are a homeowner. Particularly if you were encouraged by all the property programmes on television in recent years, to join the rush and buy either the home of your dreams, or at least a golden egg investment to make you lots of money.

Early in the recession, even the Bank of England predicted a 35 per cent drop in house prices. The property 'experts' are now divided on how long the downward trend will persist. The optimists hope for recovery in the later part of 2009. The not-so-optimistic predict a long drawn-out period of potential negative equity for some homeowners until 2023.

If you make cars it is not too good either. You are currently making too many. Global output capacity for cars is over 92 million, but sales are expected to be around just 60 million.

And unemployment during 2009 continues to rise.

The negative impact of the recession comes on top of a number of longer-term trends affecting jobs and opportunities:

You could have lost, or be about to lose your job because it might be outsourced overseas, particularly to Asia.

Your job function might be automated. A white collar worker is just as vulnerable now as was the Luddite textile weaver of the 19th century.

Your local shop might finally succumb to 'Tesconomics', where high street stores, such as Woolworths, are finally sunk by the impact of superstore chains.

And there's still the spectre of global warming hanging over us.

It all seems to add up to bad situation.

Our sensational times: the good news
For any downside there invariably is an upside.

There are unprecedented amounts of public investment being made by Governments around the world.

If you want to buy on the stock market, shares during 2009 have been relatively as cheap as they were in September 1940, at the height of Battle of Britain. If you want to buy low, now may be a good time.

Interest rates are at a 350 year low.

For first time home buyers house prices are now more affordable.

It being a buyers' market you can get some great deals out there.

I once owned an Aston Martin. (Well OK, it was a Corgi children's toy version, a best seller in 1965). But if I wanted to buy the real thing, the Big Boy's version I could save a staggering £20,000 on its pre-recession price.

There's a lot of people out there on secure incomes (well that is at least how it seems to them). Over the next year or so, they will find their weekly grocery bills, the cost of filling a tank of petrol, and lots more, cheaper. With this new extra disposable income it potentially means they have more money to spend, or to pass on to someone else in some way.

When a retail chain or store closes, its customers don't disappear. Traders left standing will get more business, be able to expand and grow and hire people - as the example of Wellworths will hopefully prove.

This is the first recession where we have the Internet. What impact will that have? The answer is, we simply don't know, but it is a new dimension with potential positive opportunities.

Looking ahead we will witness over next decade even more new, disruptive technologies. We are likely to see an 'Einstein Correction', where the very basis of our intellectual framework will be torn-up, rewritten in some way.

These changes will bring new opportunities in their wake. In much the same way how the process of bringing this book to you has been transformed - through new ways of production, such as desk top technology and the Internet - new enablers will give you new ways of doing when creating your own green shoot.

Even tackling climate change could bring opportunities for you.

Other new changes will create 'fastercheaperbetter' in some way; new opportunities for some one to take advantage of. That someone could be you.

And there's also the 'simply don't know factor'.

As financial expert John Maudlin in his blog describes: *"In 1978, in the midst of high inflation, bear markets, and malaise about all our jobs going overseas, the correct answer to the question '"Where will all the needed new jobs come from?" was "I don't know, but they will." That is the correct answer today. That is what free markets and capitalism do. They find a way to make new paths and new businesses where none existed before. And it will happen again. Just with a little lag this time."*

History is littered with examples of experts who failed to recognise the significance of computers, the Beatles, electronic watches – and Pot Noodles.

So for every cloud - even in sensational times - there is a silver lining.

More sensationalism

The term 'Sensational' is also used to describe something as exaggerated, over-inflated, lurid, making loud pronouncements on the flimsiest of texts. The dictionary chose to include the example of 'sensational journalism'.

In the same way there has been positive reaction by the UK media to feelgood good news stories any negative media coverage can actually be self fulfilling; the more they say it's doom and gloom, the more the reality takes this shape.

I do like the response of Jacqueline Gold, the founder of exotic lingerie and sex toys retailer Ann Summers, when she told city journalists: "*If I hear BBC's Robert Peston* [the broadcaster's business editor] *imply that he has 'told us so' one more time without acknowledging that the media and financial correspondents in particular have been complicit in the crushing of our customers' confidence, I will be tempted to introduce him personally to some of our more intimate products.*"

Regardless of whether you use a sex toy to respond to what you perceive as a one sided, self-fulfilling media coverage, we need to also recognise this is the first global recession of the instant 24 hour news media world.

There is an inevitable preoccupation of news media to focus on the now and immediate. The journalists then further report on what they see as a next logical step to the news development they are announcing.

In its snapshot offerings and logical extrapolations, where it reports 'a fact' and then assumes there will be one consequent scenario, the media has been guilty of making loud pronouncements without thinking through wider dimensions and implications.

It is interesting how in the English language we have

the phrase, 'a harbinger of doom' but not 'a harbinger of good tidings'. So maybe, it's an age-old thing of negative news broadcasting.

In my work I help improve people's flexible and creative thinking skills. One exercise in my creativity classes is where I give delegates a sheet of paper. I ask them to close their eyes and follow my precise instructions: folding the paper in half, tear the top left corner, fold the paper again and tear the bottom left corner.

When the class open up their eyes and unfold their sheets of paper, invariably, in spite of the clear, precise common instructions, everyone has a different shaped pattern on their paper.

The exercise highlights how the slightest variation at every step of a path can lead to countless variations. That's how nature works. That's how the future is created; many, many small steps with tiny variations at every stage creating a multitude of complexity. A butterfly flaps its wings and the weather is changed forever.

No one can predict the future. No one knows what precisely is going to happen next; no one, not the experts, not Robert Peston, not you.

So at times the news coverage really has been 'sensational' reporting specific news items of making loud pronouncements assuming there is only one course of action as a result of their latest black news.

Even more sensational

Again referring back to the dictionary, there is a third meaning to the word 'sensational'. It is the belief that all knowledge is acquired through the use of the senses.

We need to use all our senses – particularly our ears (as well as our intuition) - to investigate the world around us with its inherent opportunities.

This definition of 'sensational' again provides an appropriate definition for our times.

Each and every one of us has the potential to be a green shoot in the economic recovery. But to exploit your resourcefulness, it will require you to use of all your senses and talents in how you to respond to the challenge of the age of disruption.

 It truly is a sensational time we live in.

In all meanings of the word. It is a sensational time in which to make a difference to your life.

3. Green shoots – and why we need to spin them

The Challenge: *If you say there are green shoots out there, you will be ridiculed*

The Opportunity: *Become an individual green shoot to prove them wrong*

There is a phrase used to describe positive, new developments that will lead to a better, more prosperous future. The phrase is 'green shoots' to represent economic recovery.

It's a nice metaphor to symbolize the new, the act of renewal.

It's also a very tainted phrase.

Any utterance of the phrase is almost like creating an invitation to be shot down in a barrage of negative publicity.

The phrase was made infamous in 1991 by Norman Lamont, the then UK Chancellor of the Exchequer when he declared: *"The green shoots of economic spring are appearing once again."* Lamont used the term to gee-up optimism. Instead of green shoots, it transpired he was clutching at straws.

Since then the term, 'economic green shoots' has had a bad name for anyone claiming to see them. In January 2009 the UK Labour peer Baroness Vadera was pilloried in the media for using the term.

Whether the current economic climate is termed merely a

downturn in the economic cycle or the result of structural shifts in the economy, whether it's cyclo, structural, cyclo-structural, structural-cyclo, post dot com bubble-post house price bubble, or whatever other name you care to pin upon it, no one really knows at this stage.

One fundamental about economic history is that every downturn is at some point followed by an Upturn. In some cases the downturn can be very short, in others can be extremely lengthy. But if it is down, it will go inevitably go up at some point.

No one ever predicts a long war whenever hostilities are declared. 'Back home by Christmas' seems to be optimism prevalent both in warfare and when initially facing economic downturn.

I remembered taking some comfort from one financial expert's forecast who predicted in the spring of 2008 a double dip recession during the year, shaped like the letter 'W' with an upward path to the graph by the autumn.

It seemed to turn out be more like a '!' followed by a '?' than a 'W'.

Yes, as the downturn continues, hopes and optimism can get ground down.

Yet, any future economic historian looking back to January 2009, when Baroness Vadera made her pronouncement of 'green shoots', would be able to identify the green shoots of what led to the eventual Upturn; whether it is three months, six months, a year, several years, or decades away.

The engine for change, the seeds for recovery are evident in hindsight, even in the deepest trough of an economic cycle.

But what are we witnessing now? Queues of people waiting to beat anyone up who is predicting a positive Upturn, or at least any positive element or indication in the current climate.

Norman Lamont perhaps was guilty of spin.

And the word 'spin' gets a bad press. It implies the spinner is lying, seeking to wilfully misrepresent the truth for his or her own ends.

Yet we are all 'spinners' or 'spin doctors' (or masters of rotational medicine as the Welsh politician Rhodri Morgan called them.)

When confronted with a glass, where 50 per cent of its volume is filled with water, we invariably say the glass is either half full, or half empty: we don't have the confidence to declare it exactly 50 per cent. As a result, we will minimise or maximise the significance of any reality before us; we 'spin' our reality.

There is an inherent problem of green shoots not being able to bear the burden placed upon them, that the term itself has become jaded or misused. Indeed, in a survey conducted for this book, 95 per cent of public relations professionals declared they would not use the term 'green shoots of recovery' when making a positive statement about their organization's performance.

We have, it seems, new taboo words in the English

vocabulary. You have to be very careful before you utter 'green shoots of recovery'.

We need to use the tactics of spin as constructive tools to help in our quest to be more resourceful in the downturn.

The term 'green shoots' is not solely defined as a generic, a general wide-ranging mood, nor as a reality of economic feelgood'.

Instead, it should be usefully used as a specific, to describe an individual seed and green shoot. Possibly you.

The term 'green shoot' is about ensuring how your seed of opportunity, with the right nourishment, TLC, and determination can flower to bring further opportunities, and a new reality for you.

Being a green shoot is about creating a new positive opportunity for you. It may be doing the thing you have always wanted to do. Or responding to a negative situation not of your making, but making a positive from it – like Claire Robertson of Wellworths.

And it's not necessarily all about starting a new business or making stacks of money. It could be about getting a new balance in your life, or investing in relationships.

Whatever direction you want to take or journey you are seeking to make, it's about fulfilling your potential, making the most of your available talents and the chances that come your way.

Rather than wait for someone else to rescue you, with a statement that green shoots of recovery are arriving, you need to focus on what green shoot you can personally cultivate and deliver, to make a better future for yourself.

Your green shoot, along with those of many other individuals, may then add up to a new harvest, a collective Upturn out of the recession – the 'green shoots of recovery'.

When the business guru John Maudlin talks about not really knowing where new jobs are going to come from in a recovery – 'but they will', in essence he is describing how a multitude of economic seeds, created by people like you and me, grow, and come good.

Because these seeds are initially germinating underground, they are out of sight. If you are looking for visible evidence of these 'green shoots of recovery' you will be disappointed.

These seeds produce no immediate statistics, so there is no readily available data on the 'seeds of green shoots'. As a result, they remain invisible to the media, the world at large, but are there nonetheless, and could be visible to you - when you look in the mirror.

The future will be created by many, many different elements coming together, mostly unplanned. By using your flexible and creative thinking skills, being as resourceful as possible, by harnessing what we will later discover in this book as your small, big and different box thinking, you will recognise the potential seeds of opportunity around you.

By taking advantage, seizing the disruption, you can overcome the challenges and seize the opportunities. You can ensure you can be a green shoot and play your part in the wider Upturn of the world economy.

Whatever route, career path, lifestyle change you take, the first step in a journey of being a green shoot is to think differently. Yet, given all the negative economic news is it possible to see any positives?

If we are seeking to become a green shoot, do we need to put your current economic woes into a bigger perspective?

4. The Good News about the Black Death

The Challenge: *There's lots of bad things that can happen to you*

The Opportunity: *Your ancestors have coped with bad things – so can you (and you don't have much time left!)*

Whatever the bad news you hear about the economy there's a need for some perspective, both on a personal and historical level.

Seeing things in a bigger context, can give you a better view of your situation. It can help your resourcefulness by providing a bigger field of vision, so you can see more options and alternatives.

A personal perspective

How would you rate any problem you face created by the economic downturn on a scale of 1-10 where 9 = death (A score of 10 is for something you cherish more than yourself – a loss of a child, or some ideal you hold dear).

Whatever problem you face caused by this downturn - the loss of a job, savings ravaged, a business opportunity dashed - how does it rate?

Are you scoring 8 out of 10 at most? Or is it, in reality, much lower than this? I suspect any problem you are facing is likely to be in the low to middling, a one to seven on the perspective scale of what life can throw at you.

Now imagine a row of eight people standing in front of you.

Each person represents a different day of the week. Each day of the week represents a decade in your life, like the table below:

Person 1	Monday	0 - 10 years
Person 2	Tuesday	11 – 20 years
Person 3	Wednesday	21 – 30 years
Person 4	Thursday	31 – 40 years
Person 5	Friday	41 – 50 years
Person 6	Saturday	51 – 60 years
Person 7	Sunday	61 – 70 years
Person 8	Bank Holiday Monday	71 – 80 years

Which day of the week represents your age?

Although life expectancy beyond 80 is extending for some your lifespan will likely to be within these eight decades (or a bit beyond if there was a Bank Holiday Tuesday).

How many days of the week left do you have to see through the rest of your life? Can you afford to waste any of them by moping around, feeling miserable about any perceived current misfortune?

What's the best strategy? To moan about how bad today is, how the downturn is not fair, and how you are suffering. Or are you better served, being more constructive, creating a better destiny for yourself, by making the most of whatever time you have left on this planet?

A bigger timeframe

Bad times are nothing new. History is a chronicle of different bad times through the years.

They don't come much worse than the Black Death.

It is thought to have wiped out anything between 30-60 per cent of Europe's population in the 14th century

The fascinating and curious thing you find when you study history are the parallels you find identify between one era and another. Even our current disdain and contempt for the contemporary fat cats of our age, the bankers with their bloated bonus culture has its parallels.

The historian Simon Schama takes up the story in his 'A History of Britain'*: "The Black Death was a knock-out blow to a world that was already hurting. Paradoxically, fourteenth century England (and the rest of Britain) was a victim of its earlier success. The humming economy of the twelfth and thirteenth century had triggered a population explosion, nearly trebling the pre-Conquest population of England to around 4 million by 1300.*

The differences between the village fat cats – the men who were the jurors and ale-tasters, who worked with the reeve and owned many rather than a few strips, and who now pounced on their opportunity – and the poor village mice became more and more marked."

Yet, in spite of its massive number of deaths, the sheer misery and personal tragedies the Black Death undoubtedly brought, it may not necessarily have been all bad news.

Simon Schama again, fleshes out the story: *"Looking beyond the immediate trauma, many [historians] have concluded that in the villages, the plague was not so much the great reaper, obliterating rural life from top to bottom, [but rather] as a winnower, sorting viable from unviable communities, killing off hamlets that had already been weakened and thinned out by the hard times of the early fourteenth century."*

He adds: *"A momentous change was under way in the villages of England, Wales, and Scotland. The balance of economic power was shifting dramatically and, for once it favoured the people not the lords.*

The countryside of late mediaeval Britain was unquestionably an irreversible altered world. For one thing, it had no more serfs. For some time it had been harder to force unfree peasants to do unpaid work for their lord – to cart hay or plough fields, for example, merely in recognition of a legal right to occupy their house and yard – but now, when the laws of supply and demand so obviously favoured the survivors, it was virtually impossible. To a lord's or reeve's demand that certain tasks be done, the peasant could respond by demanding to be paid, or paid at a higher rate than before.

King Death was, then, an unlikely liberator, shaking up the old social hierarchy in the countryside and rearranging the relationship between the powerful and the powerless."

So, thanks to the Black Death your ancestors and mine were probably better off in some ways.

They were no longer serfs.

And really, a key legacy is how we are now alive, able to share this story and proclaim:

MY ANCESTORS SURVIVED THE BLACK DEATH

(Well, they lived long enough to pass on their DNA to another generation.)

So, our current situation consists of a short-term reality, which sits within the longer term, continuous thread of our history.

Your reality exists on a number of different levels.

Whatever doom and gloom is coming across on screen, on air, online or in newsprint there is deeper, longer-term news that our ancestors survived the grimmest of realities, the Black Death.

Perhaps the BBC should instruct all their business reporters to wear a special T-shirt. Imagine the BBC's Robert Peston (sans sex aid please), whenever there is a breaking story about some bank or company facing closure, about a Government borrowing unprecedented amounts of money, having to wear a T-shirt which says in big bold letters:

MY ANCESTORS SURVIVED THE BLACK DEATH

Maybe that's just a flight of fancy and most unlikely in reality, but there's nothing to stop you at least being mindful of the many different dimensions within which your reality operates.

Both the immediate bad news and the longer-term context of your ancestor surviving the Black Death are equally true, they just co-exist in different timeframes. If you solely focus on the immediate, the now, you are failing to recognise the wider truth, failing to put the immediate into a more tolerable and supportive context for you.

By recognizing your debt, not the one to the banks, but to your ancestors, you can start using them as inspirational role models to help guide you through the challenges you now face: if they can survive the Black Death, the least you can do is actively respond to the different circumstances you face, and also leave a more positive legacy for your own ancestors.

By invoking the memory of your ancestors you will never be alone.

If they can do amazing things, like surviving the Black Death, whatever is thrown at you in this recession and whatever obstacles you face in being part of the Upturn, they just do not compare with the challenges your ancestors faced in order to survive.

Go do them proud.

Your descendants may one day celebrate you becoming a green shoot by wearing a T-shirt declaring:

MY ANCESTORS SURVIVED
THE ECONOMIC RECESSION OF 2008+
(and played a part in its Upturn!)

5. Bottoms up first

The Challenge: *Other people see the world from the top down*

The Opportunity: *You can gain by looking from the bottom up*

One problem for anyone looking out for green shoots of recovery is that any shoots will grow from seeds germinating underground. As a result, they are out of sight.

A further difficulty is that you may be looking from the wrong vantage point.

Imagine if you were to create an identity parade of the world's most famous people, celebrities, or nonebrities. You would think they would be easy to spot - instantly recognizable by their fame.

If however, instead of looking at this identity parade face on, you chose to examine it directly above, so all you could see in effect is the crown of their heads and shoulders. You will find it impossible to identify them with 100 per cent certainty.

They are still famous people but your vantage point is not conducive to making an intelligent observation of the scene, or indeed for spotting the obvious.

Yet it is the very position most experts and decision-makers take when they are viewing our world of economic slowdown.

This is the look out position of the journalists, politicians, and bankers. They are looking at things top down. Their worldview is from above, not from the bottom or sides where a fuller and more realistic picture could be gained.

Most of our policy making in the UK is made top down.

Yet the real world doesn't work like that. If you wanted to examine something significant, such as how cities are created, or even something trivial like the design of minicab offices or the abundance of kebab shops in rundown parts of the UK, there is a key dynamic at work.

Why do we have cities and towns in the UK's with poorer districts, and posher areas? Has there been a strict zoning policy introduced by the local authority determining where the poor and rich people should live?

No. These areas have grown up with their location, extent and size shaped by their environment.

Richer people will have the economic freedom to move into what they perceive as the nicer, more advantageous area. Other people may decide they want to live near other richer people. And the people who don't have this freedom of choice end up being concentrated together by their circumstances.

Hey presto, over a period of time, you then get a working glass ghetto or a posh suburb.

Why is it that nearly every minicab office you visit in the UK looks the same? Have they all been slavishly following the 'Ministry of Minicabs' design guidelines for their offices, or are they just following the same environmental conditions creating similar outcomes?

Typically, a minicab office operates within a highly competitive environment and will want to pay low rent to keep their overheads as low as possible. Yet they also need to be near their customers. An important segment is late night revellers. So the likelihood is that the minicab office will be in a run down part of town, close to any vibrant nightlife.

Again keeping costs down, offices will be furnished with the bare minimum using the lowest cost, lowest maintenance materials to furnish them. The drivers need somewhere to sit in between fares. This results in a room with old settees or chairs, bare uncovered walls, and so on.

I coined the term 'kebabonomics' to describe how kebab shops are retail businesses which flourish in numbers in inner city, or deprived areas in the UK.

The reasons are again down to emergence factors; it requires low cost, easy-to- get-out-of short-term leases, using an unskilled workforce, with limited capital investment, where either a relative, or someone you know, has had direct experience of this type of business, and provides an established need for quick, available food.

This growing up from the bottom development is called 'emergence', where patterns arise out of a multiplicity of relatively simple interactions.

One big advantage you will already have over the experts is that you will be looking at the world from a different perspective; where you can see things they, and others, don't.

Your way forward is not about waiting for a top-down solution; a white knight to ride up and rescue you, presenting you with your green shoots of recovery on a platter.

Your way forward is with your bottom, or more precisely your bottom-up thinking.

Imagine you are standing at the very top of a pyramid of people. Who is there immediately to your left, right, front or back of you? There's no one. Those at the bottom are surrounded by people. If they want to do something, or immediately connect with some one, they have many more options, literally at hand. There are more people from whom to learn from and gain new information, or create new sparks of activity with.

Without bottom up thinking it is like putting a seed on a pedestal and expecting it to grow.

Surround it with appropriate nutrients and a supportive environment however, and watch it grow.

By using your flexible and creative thinking skills, harnessing whatever is around you, or available to you, your seed can grow more readily from the bottom up.

Your bottom up thinking can take advantage of immediate resources around you. It also enables you to do some that I call in Chapter 13 'Different Box

Thinking', seeing things from a different perspective
to others. It gives you the chance to create something
which others cannot, or can only do with more difficulty.

If you are seeing things differently to others it provides
you with a chance to spot your unique breakthrough
opportunities. For those at the top, they too can benefit
from having their world turned upside down.

A friend of mine asked me about Barack Obama and how
he fitted into the narrative of my story of the Upturn,
and how each and every one of us has a role to play in it
by becoming a green shoot in the recovery?

On reflection, I feel Obama is both a positive and
negative opportunity. The negative is that with his great
charisma and evident leadership skills it may encourage
some to believe he represents the solution to their
problems; his magic wand will provide an answer. The
danger is that they could wait for a solution to come to
them from him, top down.

The plus side is he represents a positive role model, a
living story of someone overcoming adversity, to reach
the pinnacle of power. If he can do it, so can you at
whatever challenge you face. Obama's key qualities it
seems to me, is his confidence in himself, a belief that
he is a man with a destiny, and that destiny is to be
President of the United States of America. Likewise, you
should have a confidence of being a green shoot in the
Upturn.

From the bottom up, in your quest to become a green
shoot, you can aim to reach the stars - or the Stars and
Stripes in Obama's case.

6. Nocebos

The Challenge: *You can make yourself ill*

The Opportunity: *You can make yourself better*

I teach creative and flexible thinking classes. People can pay me a lot of money to help them see their world differently, to come up with and deliver new ways of doing.

Two big challenges facing me in this work is getting people who are, in reality, quite-comfortable-with-the-way-as-it-is-thank-you, to change.

I have rarely met anyone who is not busy, or at least perceive they are busy. (Parkinson's First Law states how activity will always fill a vacuum, so 'busy-ness' consumes any vacuum of available time.)

The reality is that even the most modest of people suffer from hubris, an arrogance of feel they don't really need to change their status quo. They are still getting their salaries, or flow of income. There are other jobs to go to if their current one is not working out. And heck, they are REALLY busy at work, you know.

A second challenge is that once people do start reframing their existence, how you get them to follow-through, to make the ideas happen, to capitalise on any breakthroughs generated.

Even with good intentions, when they actively want to implement the ideas generated, they may find that when getting back to the office, the routine, the 'normal' takes over, and they are not much further down the line of a journey to a new world.

The great songwriter Sammy Kahn, who penned the words and music to many great songs and musicals including *'Three coins in a fountain'* was once asked a question by a fan. Intrigued about where Sammy got his creative inspiration he asked: *"Sammy, what comes first in your head when you're writing a song? Is it the words or the tune?"*

"Neither" replied Sammy. *"It's the cheque through the letterbox."*

Perhaps Sammy was a tad facetious in his reply. Yet for many people, they have been receiving their equivalent of cheques through the letterbox to stand still, not to be creative, not to challenge the status quo, but to keep doing the 'normal'.

With the economic downturn the 'normal' is no longer a norm. You don't have the option to keep doing the same thing. The cheque may not be coming through the letterbox.

It's not just a case of the goalposts being moved. Someone has taken the stadium away, and in some cases, the ball with it.

The biggest redundancy of our times is not of people and jobs.

It is the way we think: our usual boxes for thinking are redundant. They are out of date, outmoded, but still out there.

What is needed is a new way of thinking; new ways to deal with your situation and tackle whatever comes your way.

Now if the world around has you changed, this automatically creates different box thinking for you. You may have stood still but the world has dramatically moved on.

So you would think it would therefore be easy too get people to different box think.

But no.

The rabbit will often stare at the headlights of the oncoming car rather than move away.

Health experts have identified the concept of 'nocebo' – a negative twin of a placebo. Unlike a placebo, which can encourage patients to get better by believing they are having appropriate treatment, a nocebo is a self-fulfilling prophecy that you will get ill, or that your condition will worsen.

A nocebo works like this. You are told there is a problem. The problem will have a number of symptoms. All sorts of things may manifest themselves, which normally would be innocuous, but you now interpret these as the first signs of the lurgy you have been warned about.

You then start defining your life as having this condition and it now becomes a new negative reality for you. An illness has been created by your negative thought.

When it comes to the global credit crunch it seems we

have all been overdosing on 'economic nocebos' – stark warning after stark warning about economic problems - all with highly negative consequent scenarios painted.

This is not to say there aren't any problems and we should just ignore them. But how the way the story been presented in this 24 hour news media world - and the way we are reacting – can actually lead us to create a negative reality for ourselves.

Possessing, or even better, reading this book is at the very least a placebo. You may feel you are doing something constructive to address the downturn. And you may feel good reading it.

Not only is this the first recession with the Internet, it is also the first recession where we have so much knowledge and understanding about positive psychology.

Unlike previous recessions we now know much more about how to motivate and manage our mental states – like our understanding of placebos and nocebos. This book is part of this greater understanding, written to share with you and support you and others like you.

Positive psychology has provided new insights into what actually makes us happy.

If you were to offer someone the choice of having four weeks holiday when everyone else is having five weeks, or the option of three weeks holiday when everyone else is having two weeks, what do you think people typically choose?

The answer is the second option, even though you are in real terms, worse off by having less holiday time. It seems that people define what they want from life in relation to others; if others are worse off than you it seems to give you a sense of satisfaction. Your happiness is not fuelled by what you have immediately at hand, but often how you see it in relation to other people. This shapes your perception of what you see as your 'fair share'.

One curious twist to the downturn is that your happiness may be enhanced if you perceive others to be worse off than you.

We now know much more about how to cultivate and manage our mindsets in response to new challenges (again this book is one example of this).

There are even theories arguing how positive emotions have had a grand purpose in evolution, by broadening our abiding intellectual, physical, and social resources to build up reserves to draw upon in times of threats or opportunities.

When we are in a positive mood, people like us better. Friendships, new coalitions of allies are more likely to emerge as a result. When your mental mindset is expansive – it is using Bigger Box Thinking - you are more tolerant and receptive to new ideas and experiences.

Researchers have shown how in simple experiments, like giving test candidates a small bag of sweets at the beginning of the trial can, create a small blip of good feeling which leads to improved performance in creating or discovering unconventional solutions.

This book is, in a way, your equivalent of the small bag of sweets. It will make you feel more positive and comfortable with your present and as a consequence, make you more receptive to taking unconventional next steps in order to 'seize the disruption'.

It will also provide you with a range of strategies to help you make the most of your potential and also discard the habit of expecting to receive a cheque just for standing still.

Creative industries writer Richard Florida observed how a time traveller from 1900 would be amazed at the technological changes they would witness visiting a city of 1950, with the advent of the motor car and aeroplane being two obvious differences. The same time traveller moving on a further 50 years would recognise much that is familiar to them from the world of 1950, with just changes in the styling and look of cars, planes and buildings.

What probably would surprise them most about the world of 2000 would be the sociological changes they would witness, such as the changing role of women in society, and greater racial equality.

What changes would the visitor to 2050 notice?

Perhaps the next big change, in my view, is how people will have far greater understanding of their own and other people's intra-personal skills, the ability to read themselves and other people far better.

We are already significantly better at understanding what shapes and drives people's thoughts, behaviours and attitudes, but in years to come, this will increase even more markedly. It is this that will be the striking difference between future generations and us.

As my elder daughter said to me when she was just twelve years old: *"Dad, I hate it when you use reverse psychology on me!"* Getting over my initial bafflement, asking what exactly was 'reverse psychology? I then mused what will her children be saying to her?

Can we use this knowledge and insight of positive psychology to now help in your quest to become a green shoot so you can play your part in the Upturn?

7. Are we turning German?

The Challenge: *Everyone is conforming*

The Opportunity: *You can rebel*

A cornerstone belief of mine is that we are all brilliant, flexible thinking machines. On top of our shoulders is a creativity factory, also known as our brain. These particular factory units contain 100 billion cells. We create new thoughts and ideas from neuron activity when these cells connect with each other.

If you work out the maths and calculate the number of potential connections it apparently comes to 1 quadrillion 1,000,000,000,000,000. (It sounds a bit like some of the figures used on how much public money has been spent to bail out the banks.)

That's what I call a literally mind-boggling statistic.

Our brains have two modes of functioning. These modes have been given a number of names including System 1 and System 2 thinking, or our automatic and reflective systems.

I prefer to call them our Red and Green Light Thinking.

Our Red Light thinking is our logical, analytical mode, where one step logically flows into another.
In contrast, our Green Light Thinking is uncontrolled, works through making associated connections rather than a direct line and as a result can be faster and more immediate.

If you were a cook using Red Light thinking, you would strictly follow a recipe that you have researched and that you judge to be best suited to your needs.

The Green Light thinking cook in contrast, would reach out for whatever is around them, following their gut instincts, adding and spicing in whatever they intuitively felt to be best.

The great news is we can be brilliant in both dimensions.

In the first instance, we all like rules – some people more than others. So, we are all great Red Light Thinkers. (Next time you are at your gym, or parking your car think about how irritated you can be if someone has what you perceive to be your locker or your parking spot.)

When it comes to our Green Light Thinking we are equally brilliant. Let's define Green Light thinking as 'future visualization', our ability to use our imagination to create new imaginary futures – which describes any task seeking to create a new idea.

Do you have a first class honours degree from Harvard University in 'future visualization'? I suspect not.

Let me redefine the question. Are you any good at worrying? If there were a university course in 'Worrying' would you probably get first class honours degree? Would you need to do much work or revision for such a course?

Yet what is a worry? A worry is a creative act. It is a form of future visualization: you have a bit of information and your mind takes over and creates a series of imaginary scenarios resulting from this original bit of information.

What you have worried about has not actually happened. You have created it in your mind. I went through a period of refusing to listen to the radio news in the morning as it used to depress me. I would hear the latest pronouncement of doom and gloom and without realizing it, I had created a worry, using logical Red Light thinking to apply the bad media story to my life.

So, if you are brilliant at worrying you have all the mental equipment and ability in place to be equally brilliant at creativity.

The challenge we face is that our Green Light Thinking has grown up to respond to one field of play. The goalposts have been moved and we need to respond to the new environment.

This challenge has been made even more difficult by recent events preceding the credit crunch.

With the rapid growth in technology we are witnessing an exponential growth in information available to us. If you sit at a desk in the reading room of the British Library you are surrounding by rows of books. Every second, it's the equivalent of new bookshelves being added continuously, and at a faster rate.

The size of your desk in the library however, remains the same. So you can only accommodate a limited quota of the books. If having books arrive on your desktop was your only source of new data you would find yourself obtaining a small proportion of what is available.

We are becoming more and more expert, at narrower and narrower fields of knowledge.

To cope with this realization you can make yourself more inflexible. In spite of the growing technological smartness, the world can often appear more stupid.

The inflexible telephone call centre is a great example of phenomenal technology at work, but getting it to respond to your easy, yet off script request, can be a nightmare experience. (These experiences prompted me to write a book in 2008 called *'Overcoming Stupidity'* – I stupidly thought I ought to do something about this trend.)

Another difference is cultural.

If we are going to go on a journey, to explore how you can best think differently and respond differently to your new circumstances – and be more resourceful in the downturn - we may have to undo some recently acquired habits.

On another journey, this time on a train, I overheard a conversation between two guys, relating about the time one of them spent living and working in Germany.

When asked what the big differences were between the two countries, the former expat reflected: *"In the UK, you can do whatever you like, so long as there is not a law saying you can't do it. In Germany, you can do whatever you like, so long as there is a law that says you can do it."*

I reflected on the overheard comment: Is this more than just a neat parallel into how he perceived the cultural differences between the two European countries? In fact, how up-to-date is his comment? Have we in Britain move to a situation where we cannot make our minds for ourselves but have to be told what to do?

I am reminded of the story about the scientific experiment where common frogs if dropped into boiling water, will leap to safety, but boiled up from ambient, they will simply cook.

Have we been slow to respond to changes in our culture where we have prevailing principles of doing whatever we want to do, so long as there is a law saying you can't do it?

Have we witnessed in the UK a growth in conformist thinking, rather than a culture of freely pursuing new things without having to be given orders or permission to do so?

The growth in 'healthandsafetyitus', where the very laudable concept and practice of 'health and safety' has been applied to seemingly ludicrous lengths is an obvious expression of this trend.

A specific example is the increase in the number of hung juries witnessed in the UK.

In the last two years the number of hung juries - where no verdict is reached - has more than doubled. There were just 52 hung juries in England and Wales in 2006. Yet in just two years, by 2008, the figure had more than doubled with 116 hung juries.

A hung jury is usually a recipe for bad news; the defendant face ongoing anxiety and uncertainty, witnesses may face having to give traumatic evidence again, while the taxpayer will have to pay for any future retrial. Hung juries cost the taxpayer nearly £30 million in 2008.

It appears to be symptomatic of changes in our society, where people are much more nervous about being judgmental, wanting all the boxes ticked before giving a final assent. It is also a symptom of what is called the 'CSI effect', where forensic evidence is now more significant part of trials.

Popular television shows such as the CSI series raise the expectations of crime victims, jury members and even criminals of forensic science, especially DNA testing and crime scene investigation.   Much of this faith is actually inspired by the creative licence of the shows' writers which overstate both the accuracy of the forensic techniques, and exaggerate its potential to deliver an infallible verdict.

In the face of the economic downturn we need to rewire our automatic thinking to cope with the demands of this new age. Yet we face the danger of having become a society of people who have to wait to be told what to do, rather than thinking on their own feet and being responsive to the changing times around them.

Most advice for businesses in the recession focuses on:

- Maintain your cash reserves as much as possible

- Cut down on all non-essential spending

- Focus on your core strengths

- Invest in your marketing
- Be more innovative

Apart from the strategy of being innovative the other strategies just use what is called your convergent thinking, your ability to think within known constraints. (They are essentially good housekeeping strategies that you should be doing anyway.) At best these might succeed in creating incremental change for your future where you are combining known elements to hopefully get one step ahead – or minimize any backward steps.

If you want to really flourish you need exponential change; massive, superlative growth can only come from being innovative, which uses your divergent, flexible, or creative thinking.

Certainly, the war against your divergent, flexible thinking is not new. I recall how I was the only child in the East End of London with a triple barrelled name. Two or three times a day the teachers would remind me of my triple barrelled name by saying: *"Green-Stop-Daydreaming!"*

Our schools and education system has had a tendency to teach us what to think, rather than how to think. Yet in the analogy between Britain and Germany, are we witnessing a step up in the war against creativity, with a consequent decline in flexible thinking skills?

Is our thinking environment marked by being increasingly prescriptive, following set orders from above?

Have we, like the frog in boiling water, become inured to the change in thinking temperature where we now only do what we think we are told to do? Are we losing an ability to effectively respond, so we can become a green shoot?

Or can you do something about it, to make sure you succeed in this downturn?

8. The age of disruptive opportunities

The Challenge: *There are lots of bad changes forced upon you*

The Opportunity: *You need to change anyway*

There is only one person out there who can really help you.

And that's you.

You have resources in how you think, respond and move ahead to any new situation you face.

If you can move faster, more responsive to any changes in your environment then you will have a competitive advantage. You are also operating in a world whose speed has dramatically increased.

Even to make sure you are not left behind you have to move fast. To get ahead, you need to go even faster. The old phrase *'when the going gets tough, the tough get going'* needs to be rephrased for the 21st century to:

'When the going gets tough, the tough get going faster.'

There's a wealth of academic and business school research revealing how in previous recessions market shifts are greatest in a downturn.

In a benign or growing economy successful businesses often just rely on their sheer size for success. In downturns however, people are more prepared to switch suppliers, make new decisions representing an opportunity for the agile and adaptable people to exploit new gaps in the market.

There's the great Harry Lime quote, inspired by Orson Welles, in the film 'The Third Man': *"Don't be so gloomy. After all it's not that awful. Like the fella says, in Italy for 30 years under the Borgias they had warfare, terror, murder, and bloodshed, but they produced Michelangelo, Leonardo da Vinci, and the Renaissance. In Switzerland they had brotherly love - they had 500 years of democracy and peace, and what did that produce? The cuckoo clock."*

Disruption is good for getting people to do things different. It overcomes what is called the 'status quo bias' where people tend not to change an established behavior unless the incentive to change is compelling. Guess what? With the recession they cannot rely on the status quo, the cheque coming through the letterbox, the existing way of doing. People are being forced to change.

Our current age has been compared to the 1930's Great Depression. As soon as you mention the name 'Great Depression' it conjures up iconic images of Jarrow Hunger marchers or the American images of the Dustbowl captured by photographers Arthur Rothstein and Dorthea Lange.

Yet within these hard times there was another reality.

My oldest brother lives in an attractive semi detached house in North London. His 'semi' – and the many others like it – is an iconic feature of the English streetscape, with neat rows of private houses built in the 1930's stretch for miles around London.

Some three million homes were built in the UK between 1933 and 1939 –compared to 200,000 a year at the height of one of the biggest building booms in 2007. (The role of the building societies was one key factor for this growth was. Although founded in the 1900's they took on a thriving role – especially after small depositors lost faith with banks.)

During the 1930's Britain expanded a small car industry into a huge, varied and highly efficient one, a world leader in many categories.

Britain expanded its aero-engine and airframe sector into the most innovative in Europe. It created entirely new industries in radar, electronics, pharmaceuticals and chemicals. It had some of the best experimental laboratories in the world.

In the United States the 1930s witnessed many entrepreneurial start-ups that went on to become household names such as Hewlett-Packard, Motorola, and Texas Instruments. The ubiquitous Coca Cola took become the number one soft drink brand during this period, displacing the then brand leader Moxie which had cut its advertising spend during the Great Depression

Later recessions saw the birth of modern-day success stories as diverse as Microsoft, South-West Airlines, MTV, and Ben & Jerry's Ice cream.

All these positives at times we usually associate with negative doom and gloom.

What will economic historians of the future look back to

the world of 2009 and celebrate their growth, success as an engine for the economy of the future?

Booms in 2009 are already currently being reported in products ranging from frozen pizza to museum visits.

Everyone has his or her own experience of a recession. Some do badly. Others do very well. The gloomy averages fail to convey the true range of experiences. The definition of a recession is actually a statistical average.

A business survey during 2009 (Blue Sheep Oxford Economics, March 2009) confirms how our reality is not a case of one size fits all.

True, the overall picture has dramatically changed year on year; with sectors previously enjoying robust healthy seeing a bleak future. IT and manufacturing were particularly badly hit, whereas the Transport and the Energy sectors were relatively optimistic.

There was still a strong performance showing from parts of the financial sector, reflecting the massive injection of public money as the government attempts to head off the worst of the recession.

Previous regional variations were broadly maintained, with London and the South East still outperforming other UK regions in all sectors. This was expected to carry on as Government capital projects are brought forward and spending on the 2012 Olympics continues.

In the current downturn the survey expected around one in eight companies to grow and at least 45 per cent to shrink with the rest essentially remaining static.

OK this is a negative to the picture 12 months earlier. But the results do confirm the schism, the difference in reality between the headlines in the media and the real world for many in the economy.

If your business is not growing, but neither is it losing much, that frankly is not a great news story. Yet, it reflects the reality for many. It is a reality that does not get reported. Instead, the dramatic, instantly newsworthy, negative soundbite gets the coverage.

What is problematic for traditional business is a new opportunity for others. A new green shoot opportunity possibly for you.

The good news about the age of disruption is how it actually forces people to make decisions. They have to exercise a choice as their reality has been taken away from them, with a redundancy notice or other setback.

They cannot wait for the next cheque to come through their letterbox. Someone has made the decision for them.

My friend Judi Goodwin, a freelance writer, told me her story, when her reality was transformed in a previous age of disruption.

> *"I had abandoned a career as an advertising copywriter to put my first foot on the journalism ladder, via a job in corporate comms at the CWS. It was a great job and I loved it. After three years they decided to close the department and we were made redundant.*

I was distraught. My journalism career nipped in the bud. I was 23 and had no real journalistic experience. The 'Stockport Express' turned me down. The ICI staff magazine turned me down. I felt useless and rejected. I cried buckets for weeks until the dreaded redundancy day arrived. Would I have to return to advertising which I hated?

I signed on the dole and looked around for freelance writing work to keep the money coming in. In my first week I earned more for two days work than I'd previously earned for a whole week in staff employment. OK, so I was writing ad copy. But it would get me by 'till something came along.

Slowly I began to spot freelance journalistic opportunities. The career took off. I've never looked back. I would never have had the courage and self belief to launch myself as a self employed journalist at the time, but circumstances gave me a wonderful kick up the bum.

Since then I've written for big titles like the Daily Telegraph and 'Radio Times', worked as a broadcaster/interviewer for 'Woman's Hour' and 'You and Yours', been a Consultant Commissioning editor for 'Ideal Home'- and launched a successful interiors photographic library. Andy, you know the rest."

Judi's experience is far from unique. Catching the radio show *'Woman's Hour'* on BBC Radio 4, it invited listeners to share their experiences of responding to a downturn.

There was an absolutely amazing range of responses. The lady who started a new career as an Alpaca wool farmer was particularly memorable.

In responding to the age of disruption, doing something to create your own green shoot, you don't necessarily have to do something exotic, like Alpaca wool farming. (Although that particular market may well have opportunities for you.)

As long as you do something. That is the crucial first response.

Getting fired can often be a godsend; someone else is making the decision for you. Through inertia, many people are doing a job which is not actually the best choice for them. As a result they can face a slow spiritual demise by tolerating the mediocre.

A great creativity technique I use is to get people to redefine is to state their situation as an equation such as:

$$\text{Economic downturn} \neq \text{downturn in you, or your resourcefulness}$$

Can you extend your personal equation to take into account your skills, immediate opportunities around you?

Just because the world has gone to pieces, doesn't mean you have to.

In fact it could be making of the new you.

Your green shoot could be about to grow.

9. Golden Swans

The Challenge: *Brilliant opportunities can be missed*

The Opportunity: *You can seize the brilliant opportunity*

The age of disruption is almost like a reshuffling of the pack in a game of cards. It is not an overall revolution of society. After all, in the UK we live in a country where a fifth of the land is still owned by the ancestors of the Norman invaders of 1066.

The disruption does however present opportunities for both a personal revolution in how you respond to the times and change, and also a revolution in new sectors. It gives you new cards to play with, or new cards in circulation to reshape your hand for your winning breakthrough.

Kurt Vonnegut created a character who lectured his son to be alert to a situation where two people are going to give money to each other, and advised the son how he needs to be in the middle of the transaction. It seemed to neatly capture everything you need to know about business; business is about getting between two people who are giving each other money. The age of disruption will create new situations, new niche markets and new ways to offer *fastercheaperbetter*, where you can find yourself between two people giving each other money.

The age of disruption is what the writer Nassim Nicholas Taleb calls a 'Black Swan' event where it represents an unexpected and large impact event which shapes the course of history.

He uses the analogy of a turkey reviewing its situation at the beginning of December. The turkey reflects how it has enjoyed good food, gained considerable weight and if they were able to draw a graph, would extrapolate and predict a similarly positive future.

Reality for either the turkey's real predicament at Christmas, or the path of the global economy is however, somewhat different. Instead of predictable lines providing a reassuring path for your destiny, history is characterised by seismic shifts of disruptive change.

Although Taleb does reference how there are good Black Swans - an example could be for example, the discovery of antibiotics - I feel we would be better served by making a distinction between positive and negative Swans.

We need to have 'Golden Swans'.

A 'Golden Swan' can be described as an unexpected positive major breakthrough opportunity that, if seized upon, would yield significant results.

A key reason why we need to have a specific name for 'Golden Swans' is a recurrent characteristic of people frequently being blind to them, failing to invest sufficient resource in them, or not fully capitalising on them.

Golden Swans can also be squandered by failing to take advantage of the opportunity to do something new, take a different strategic direction in your life, or a failure to avoid 'spending the kids' inheritance.'

The example of how Britain misused its oil wealth, in

contrast to its more frugal North Sea neighbour Norway is a good example; instead of spending its riches lavishly, Norway passed legislation ensuring that oil revenue went straight into its sovereign wealth fund. This fund is now the largest pension fund in Europe and the second largest in the world.

History is littered with other examples of wasted Golden Swans.

According to historian Alan Clark, during World War I the Allies succeeded in breaking through the German lines not just once, but three times. On each occasion they failed to seize the advantage and major breakthrough it could have entailed.

Back in ancient times, a man who really was a creative hero, Hero of Alexandra invented the first steam power engine. At the time, around AD50, it was thought of little more than a curiosity, rather than as a Golden Swan opportunity to bring forward the Industrial Revolution by 1,600 years.

For any Sheffield United football fans (when they are not blaming my beloved West Ham United for their plight) could also point their fingers at their club's board which had the opportunity back in 1978 to sign football legend Diego Maradona as a 17 year old, only to reject their manager's recommendation as £40,000 too expensive.

I live on Barry Island, near Cardiff which combines a beautiful coastline with the blight of a traditional British seaside resort having seen former glories.

For three years the Island has enjoyed national media profile, watched by millions of viewers thanks to its being featured in the BBC TV comedy series *'Gavin & Stacey'*. Yet, for much of this period, visitors to the resort would have been in blissful ignorance of any connection between the place and the TV series. A Golden Swan promotional opportunity went begging.

Think back on your own life. How many times did you say 'No' when you should have said 'Yes'? Or did you wish you had increased your stakes to take advantage of the winning bet?

With our 20:20 vision of hindsight, our own lives are full of 'If only…reflections'

We are now living in an age of disruption. Just as we have an obvious, very evident Black Swan event, with the current recession, our age will also contain many, many Golden Swan opportunities.

The age of the Internet is now creating the world's single biggest-ever consumer market, essentially talking the same language and using the same technology. This will be great opportunities for you. And also it offers great opportunities for others to take the bread from your mouth.

Will you again be saying 'If only…'

So how can we best be prepared, whether it is just making the negative less painful or the positive better – or even seizing a Golden Swan for your green shoot opportunity?

You first step is to think differently.

You need to build the foundations for your ability to be more resourceful, by thinking flexibly, and thinking flexibly faster in this age of disruption – so you can become a green shoot.

Going forward...

Section I described our context, the situation we now face. It outlined the need for you to think flexibly if you are to become a green shoot, to contribute to a wider Upturn.

If you wanted to create a list of attributes you require for being a 'green shoot in the Upturn', the job description could read:

> *'Upturn seeks person to become a green shoot to be innovative, be creative and think flexibly, with the ability to be self-started, take responsibility, spot opportunities, build bridges and alliances, persuade themselves and then others what they are doing is right, play a percentage game by not putting all their eggs in one basket and recognize every 'No' or slammed door in their face is a step forward, ability to bounce back from setbacks, learn from experiences, create luck for others, understand themselves - knowing what makes them tick and not tick, identify and harness their core skills, manage resources and tight budgets, stay focussed and avoid distractions from their central goal, use any and every contact, be adaptable and jump further/higher/faster than the other person, and should still keep smiling - or at least keep their own spirits up - amidst the chaos.'*

All very straight forward you might think. Most of these behaviours would match what you probably know about the characteristics of successful entrepreneurs.

But why aren't you doing this now?

What do you need to be different?

What tools do you need to bring about the change you desire?

Section II shares how you can think more flexibly by using your cocktail of different thinking skills. It reviews the resources within you. It acts as a primer for how you can give yourself a disposition to be more flexible.

The chapters each use a different metaphor to symbolise the tools in your toolbox. The section will explain how a pit stop, a bungee rope, a medal from your trophy case, beautiful boxes, and a Martini clock can be used to help you think more flexibly.

Section III highlights how in the age of disruption, you don't just need to think flexibly. You need to think flexibly faster. The section acts as a primer to give your mind the equivalent of running shoes, so you can give yourself a disposition to think flexibly faster.

Discover how a magnet, small stepladder, an elastic band, a toilet chain along with a black sock, and a sledgehammer can be your tools for thinking flexibly faster.

Section IV introduces you to Part Two of this book.

10. A pit stop for your pessimism

I hate positive thinking.

I remember having a heated discussion with a business partner discussing our business beliefs and values. My number one belief is that life is too short. *"You can't say that"* my colleague despaired: *"You have got to say 'Life is full of abundance!'"*

I didn't believe it then, nor do I believe it now.

Frankly, life is too short. What is the one resource we have that once gone we can never reclaim? If you did the 'Which day of the week represents your age' test in Chapter 4 it brings home with some clarity how we don't really have much of this thing called life.

In fact our time is the most precious resource on our planet.

The first task in being flexible in your thinking and making a contribution to the Upturn is to be pessimistic.

Pessimism is good. Research shows that pessimists are far more accurate in their judging of situations than happy people. They are sadder but wiser.

Depressed people are accurate judges of how much skills they have.

Happy people think they are more skilful than others judge them to be. Have you ever met a driver who owns up to be below average in their driving?

Happy people remember more good events than actually happened and forget more of the bad events.

Happy people are lopsided in their beliefs about success and failure.

Happy people are losers, especially if they think just in that mode during the first stage of the Upturn.

One of the major biases in risky decision-making is optimism. Optimism is a source of high-risk thinking. Groups tend to be optimistic, where the whole group suppresses doubts.

We all know the Emperor's clothes tale. Sadly, how often do we experience it and even contribute to it? Inevitably, there is a tendency and incentive to support the whole group leading to what is labelled 'groupthink'.

With the rise in conformist thinking there is even more impetus to agree in admiring the Emperor's new clothes, unless either someone tells you not to, or you decide to break the groupthink spell.

Being negative about the prevailing mode of thought, to swim against the tide requires you to think and say 'No', or 'This is not quite right', 'This is not the way to go ahead' – questions triggered by being negative and pessimistic to the prevailing orthodoxy. Your negativity, is the most crucial asset in being creative, making new things happen, and redefining your world.

This might sound paradoxical, but think of the example of a car.

Guess what is probably the most crucial part of a car to make it go as fast as possible?

Is it the engine or the tyres?

Surprisingly it's the brakes.

Knowing you have the capability to stop, control the forward surge of motion, gives you the confidence to go fast, and even faster. Without the brakes you would be cautious, tentative and slow. You might have the fastest car going but if you can't ease it's speed or bring the thing to a stop when necessary, you restrain putting your foot down on the accelerator.

The brakes on the car are the equivalent to your pessimism when making judgments.

Judgment comes from experience, and experience comes from bad judgment. You learn from your mistakes. You avoid making future mistakes by being aware of the bad things you have experienced, either first or second hand.

You need pessimism to tell you the real chances of something happening.

You need pessimism to ignore the expert advice you are being given.

You need pessimism to disagree with the crowd, the groupthink.

Pessimism is good. But not all the time.

If you lived your life in a negative mode of permanent and pervasive pessimism you would not venture out of your front door. You would always be fearful the worse would happen.

So it is obviously not an effective mode of thought if you are planning to be a seed for a green shoot to change your world.

Pessimism is an essential tool in your creative toolbox, but it needs to be used appropriately and sparingly.

On sharing this idea with a friend he said, *"Oh, so you need to be a semi-sceptic"*. I was wary of this idea. I think being a 'semi-sceptic' leads to ambiguity and uncertainty. Instead of a semi-sceptic, you need to be a total sceptic in small, concentrated doses.

You need to be flexible in your thinking, appropriately introducing pessimism when a rain check is needed.

I call this 'Pit stop Pessimism'.

The idea, like the Formula I car in a grand prix race, the visit to the pit stop is essential to maintain its wellbeing and ability to complete the race or adapt to new circumstances. Like the Formula I car you don't want to spend your whole time in the pits. You need to go in, rapidly have you reality makeover, and then get out again.

Pit stop pessimism enables you to embrace the negatives in your life, ensuring you make a realistic a judgement as possible, identifying the obstacles, the 'why-it-won't-works', and the challenges ahead. Addressing these, you can now go more purposely forward in your quest.

Many good businesses will go under during this recession, because they were unlucky with their debts. They were unlucky with the people who owed them money. They may have not been pessimistic early enough to prevent the worse happening. Paranoia can be healthy.

You are a lot more confident driver if your car is regularly checked and serviced. Your reality check through your pessimism is the equivalent of the car being serviced or quickly being checked over at the pit stop.

Pessimism is vital for your flexible thinking to give you a crucial reality check reference point. By flexibly using it, and flexibly moving away from it, will make your subsequent thinking more robust – because you have already thought of the worst possibilities, and thought through ways around them.

Pessimism, don't become a green shoot without it.

In the age of disruption you need to embrace the worst – and revisit it regularly. But there are other places you also need to go to if you want to think more flexibly in your quest to become a green shoot.

Your green shoot Action Steps

1. *Ask yourself, what are the positive assumptions you are making about your situation and plans for being a green shoot?*

2. *What positive assumptions are others making about your situation?*

3. *What can wrong with your plans for the future? What can <u>really</u> go wrong?*

4. *If the worst was to happen, what would it score in the scale of 1-10, (described in Chapter 4) with 9 remember, being your own death?*

5. *What can you do to minimise the impact of the worst case scenarios or prevent them from happening?*

11. A bungee rope for your vision

Have you ever done, or know someone who has done a bungee jump?

You essentially place your trust and belief that wherever you are going to throw yourself, you are going to have one hell of an experience – and complete trust in how you will bounce back, return to where you started, survive, and somehow how your life will be better as a result of the experience.

Being a seed for a grass shoot is a bit like doing a bungee jump, in springing forth, not quite sure where it is precisely going or what exactly is going to happen.

To become a seed of a green shoot you need to have what I call a Big Bungee Vision.

Like doing a bungee jump, you are going to do something, going somewhere different.

I would define vision as having a sense of horizon, a destination of where you want to be. The more total and real you can make your picture of what your destination like, the more it will act as a magnet to attract you towards it.

There is also another name for vision. It is called dreaming.

Dreams are wonderful.

Most people I meet are brilliant film-makers. They don't have a film-making diploma, nor are their films on celluloid or digital format.

All of us make films every night when we sleep. When you dream you are making a film. It could be a film about your past, future, anxieties or hopes.

Your film-making is so good you experience the film as being real, so it's even better than the stuff you see on telly or at the cinema.

Next time you wake up, don't try and remember the narrative, the plot of your dream. Instead try to capture the film elements of it: what was the editing like of the different scenes, the camera angles, the lighting, the locations, and particularly my dreams, the clothes!

Anyone who appears in your dreams wearing clothes has been dressed by you. (I once did a creativity course with a group of Norwegians and this real big guy puts his hand up and shares his insight in his Nordic accent: *"Most of my dreams are ov a sexual nature."* I thanked him for sharing his experience.)

You have this brilliant ability to be creative in your sleep. Just tapping into a small percentage of this when you are awake could transform your reality.

While it is important to have a vivid, coherent dream or vision, before embarking on the big leap of faith - like a bungee jump - you still need to be connected to where you are. It's almost like an insurance policy, of having a way of getting back.

The challenge in being a seed for a green shoot is you are doing the equivalent of a bungee jump; you know where you want to go with your sense of vision, and you have the confidence of your own self and the knowledge about your opportunity that you will be safe.

Without the bungee rope you are either jumping off into a possible black hole, or without its connectivity to your present you could be left just dangling and wither away.

To adapt the quote from the ancient Greek philosopher Heraclitus: *"No person steps into a bungee jump twice; each jump will be different, and the person will be changed as a result of each experience."*

I developed a theory that, at least in their own minds, people don't take risks. After all, anyone doing a bungee jump doesn't really believe they won't miss the ground and bounce back up.

I developed the idea after my experience as a young public relations executive. At the time I was working on a charity account for the spinally injured. Part of our work was to interview recent patients at the spinal injuries ward. One guy I interviewed had experienced a horrific gliding accident. He was a pilot of a glider and some one had stupidly left a rope across the runway. As his plane was towed into the air, it got entangled with the rope and come crashing down some 30ft aloft.

Looking back I was insensitive with my comment: *"You're lucky to be alive!"* To which he, glancing down at his wheelchair and a life of spinal injury replied: *"Do you call this lucky?"*

Although feeling rather stupid, I carried on with the interview. Years later I reflected about what must have going through the guy's mind when he went gliding. Did he really envisage having an accident? Did he really believe he ran the risk of an accident where he would be wheelchair bound?

My conclusion was that he embarked on being a glider pilot aware of a factual risk that there could be an accident if you are high up in the sky, in a big balsa wood construction with no engine. But the film he had in his head was of him successfully enjoying the experience and safely landing. He did not believe he would have an accident. The technical risk was a fact in his brain, but not a reality in his likely scenarios. The wheelchair was not on the props list of their *'My gliding experience'* film.

In your quest having a vision, a sense of where you want to go is valuable, whether it is taking advantage of the immediate, through to the longer term.

Like a bungee jump experience being a green shoot will be lonely; you are doing a bungee jump with the equivalent of an invisible elastic rope. You know it's there, but others can't see it.

You are about to enter a lonely world, a lonely place where frankly you may not want to enter.

The place is you doing something new.

You know you need to respond differently.

You need to take advantage of these different times.

But you need to let go.

The most powerful voice you have is a voice no one can hear. It is the voice in your head.

Don't worry the voice is not a sign of delusional behaviour. It is something we all have. It is a voice however that will hold you back, say you can't do things, and keep reminding you of how stupid you were in beginning your journey; maybe what your mother/partner/colleagues/man in the corner shop said about your idea was true.

The place you are going to doesn't have a map, a picture showing you where the next service station and how far your destination is. Your journey is not about to be guided by a Satnav telling you the best road to take and giving you strict instructions about your precise next turn, or to reassure you to keep going straight on.

You are setting forth in the frightening yet hugely stimulating and exciting world of unexpected change, pitfalls, inadequacy and more.

You do however have one extremely powerful asset. You.

The fact that you were born is a miracle of different combination of elements, circumstance and environment.

You have within you a remarkable talent to withstand setbacks, identify goals and respond and adapt to new things around you.

What if we could make the most of this talent, to expand your resourcefulness to ensure you can do something now to respond to the age of disruption?

The equivalent of the bungee jump rope in this journey is your self belief in you, your confidence in your next step, and you know what you are doing.

Many people suffer from poor quality health, in what can be called 'health excusitis'. Their poor condition is often front-of-mind, the centrepiece of conversations, and it becomes a self-fulfilling nocebo.

A strategy recommended by David J. Schwartz in his *'The magic of thinking big'* to tackle 'health excusitis' and enjoy better health is to:

- refuse to talk about your poor health
- refuse to worry about your poor health
- be genuinely grateful your health is as good as it is
- remind yourself that 'it's better to wear out than rust out'

I feel this gameplan for better health is also valid for better greenshoot wellbeing.

So to adapt the strategies and overcome the economic nocebos around you by:

- only talk about how bad things are – with yourself and others – in pit stop pessimism mode.
- refuse to be worried about bad economic prospects, or other negatives to your plans
- enjoy and be grateful for what economic wealth, standing you have at present
- remind yourself that you 'can't take it with you', a pile of gold in your coffin is not much good for you.

By having this attitude, coupled with your bungee vision, you are equipping your seed with greater resilience to go forth and become a shoot.

By having a vision – by seeing something - you are one step nearer to it. You need to think 'Big' about:

- You, your ability, your capability to make the change you want to see in the world happen.
- Your prospect of your future being bigger than your present reality
- Your making the world a different place in some way

If we define an idea as a mental concept featuring a combination of different things which together add value, make the world a different, better place in some way, the reality of your idea is just that: it is a mental concept. It is not real. It is not happening now. It needs the right nurture and opportunities to be realized.

The Big Bungee Vision is not an instant, immediate big idea.

In my work I have acted as a business mentor for numerous individuals and fledgling businesses, where I have sought to be a constructive friend, being helpful and positive where necessary, yet truthful with the facts, even if it hurts.

My alarm bells start to ring whenever I am given presentations of grandiose organization charts, a family of brand logos, and whenever I get a 'No' answer to what I feel is a fundamental question: 'Has anyone ever given you a pound for this service, or anything similar?

Far too often their vision is more like a fantasy, wishful thinking, than an effective or supportive tool rooted in supporting actions. One simple way of giving the Bungee Vision of your plans to become a green shoot a reality check is to simply toss a coin; heads you are still going ahead with your plans. Tails you abandon them. If the coin lands tails up meaning you give up the plan, but you hear the voice in your head suggesting you do another toss, then it is your intuition being articulated. It is saying 'Go ahead'.

Another useful tool is to have two visions: a low hanging fruit one – where, with some stretching you can achieve it. Alongside this you need what I call a, 'reach for the stars' vision, inspired by the quote from the great adman, Leo Burnett who said: *"When you reach for the stars you may not quite get one, but you won't come up with a handful of mud either."*

By aiming for both goals you won't beat yourself up if you fail to reach the stars, but can still motivate yourself to think the biggest thoughts.

If you want to become a successful green shoot you need a dream with a step ladder to get you there – a Big Bungee Vision - to connect with your current reality, but flexible take you to other places, some of which might even be scary.

Your flexible thinking repertoire is now expanding, where you can use, and alternate between Pit Stop Pessimism and Bungee Vision. What else do you need to add?

Your green shoot Action Steps

1. *In your plans to be a green shoot where do you want to be, is it somewhere different to where you are now*

2. *What is this different place like – what does it look, feel, smell or taste like?*

3. *How will you know you have arrived at this new place?*

4. *How can you make your Bungee Vision to be a green shoot more than a dream – how can you connect it to where you are now?*

5. *What are your 'low hanging fruit' or 'reach for the stars' goals? Toss a coin now to decide if you are going ahead with your plans to become a green shoot*

12. A medal from your medal case

No matter how strong and potent your vision is, you will inevitably run into obstacles - potential barriers that prevent you from reaching where you want to be. The greatest skill of a potential green shoot is not to give in.

The films *'Rocky'* and *'The Shawshank Redemption'* feature inspirational characters who despite handicaps, knock-backs and knockdowns, fulfil their dreams.

You might be familiar with Intelligence Quotient (IQ), your ability to rationalise and be logical. You may also be familiar with your Emotional Quotient, your ability to understand emotions and intra and inter personal empathy.

Your most important quotient however, when it comes to your flexible and creative thinking is another dimension. It is your Adversity Quotient, your will to succeed, your resilience, the ability to bounce back, not be deterred in your quest. Everyone has setbacks; the successful green shoot overcomes these.

If you want to be a green shoot, it's down to you.

Successful green shoots will be 100 per cent accountable. Inevitably, they will face setbacks. They respond by making themselves 100 per cent accountable for dealing with their problems.

They have a high Adversity Quotient.

A good friend of mine is leading motivational speaker Steve McDermott. He frequently asks his audiences: *'What percentage of your life's success is down to you and what percentage is down to things you have no control over – such as luck, class, circumstances?'*

An audience made up of executives reply with a figure usually around 80 per cent; 80 per cent is down to them, 20 per cent they have no control over.

Steve's response is they need to be 100 per cent accountable. Successful people have setbacks but make themselves completely accountable for doing something about it.

Inspired by Steve, I got him, as part of an urban regeneration initiative, to speak at an event for council estate representatives. We thought when asked the same question they might come up with a slightly lower figure than 80 per cent.

Their response was startling. In fact it was a completely inverse to the executives: the people on the council estate thought they had just 20 per cent control over their future destiny. Millions of pounds had been spent on bricks and mortar in the regeneration initiative, but nothing on the minds and attitudes of the people. As soon as something goes wrong the people do not see themselves as accountable for doing anything about it.

This is a true story from the same housing estate. There was a big queue at the Housing Association's office where tenants reported any repairs and maintenance jobs for their properties. A guy dutifully waited his turn and when he got to the desk and was asked how could he be helped, he replied: *"My flat is on fire."*

The man with the burning flat had lost the self-responsibility to take appropriate action for his situation.

He had acquired what is called 'learned helplessness'. Conditioned by negative responses in his life he seemingly learnt that whatever you do, you cannot get, and eventually learns to give up.

It might be easy to mock or sneer at people with extreme learned helplessness but all of us have some aspect of victim mentality.

Learned helplessness is not jus an overall mindset but can work in silos of our thinking, or in certain aspects of your life.

My wife sometimes remarks that I am so positive I sometimes 'piss people off with my optimism'. It is true in many aspects of my life- whether it having view that that we are all potential green shoots in the recession and how it can provide positive Golden Swan opportunities – I am positive.

Like the time I reflected that somehow 'the world was getting more stupid', and decided to do something about this by launching the Stupid Aid campaign and writing a book, *'Overcoming Stupidity'*; is this a sign of someone who sees themselves as helpless?

Yet, in other aspects of my life I have beliefs which are not positive. I somehow think it is not fair that I weigh more than I would ideally like. It's almost like I have an affliction where I put on weight by looking at food.

Similarly, when it comes to my beloved football team, West Ham United (club motto: *'We lose some, we draw some'*) I have a similar negativity as soon as the opposition get the ball in our half.

How many of us have silos of negative thinking or even learned helplessness when responding to negatives about the global economy, the impact on your organization, job or life?

Who is responsible for putting us in this negative situation? The bankers? Well, sure they created the financial mess. But they are not the ones holding you back in how you choose to respond to it.

Is it the politicians with their failure to properly regulate and control the excesses of the financial 'wild party'? Sure, they take some responsibility for the cause. But in terms of your response, that is down to you.

While you cannot and should not be 100 per cent accountable for things you don't have 100 per cent control of, there is no such excuse when it comes to you and how you respond to the age of disruption.

You have 100 per cent control of you.

Are you going to take responsibility and make a 100 per cent response to your new situation?

But, it's got to mean something if you want it to really happen.

In order to achieve any success in any task in your life it must have meaning. Whenever I give a talk, in my mind

I have dedicated it to someone I respect in order to give the task deeper meaning.

The writer Douglas Adams in the last years of his life suffered a major writer's block. He had secured a multi-million publishing deal yet the words for his book would not flow, would not come to him. Adams had figured the number of words required for the book and even estimated a cash figure for each word.

Having enjoyed success with his various *'Hitchhikers Guides to the Galaxy'* books Adams savoured a good lifestyle in California. He was evidently not driven or motivated by money. In his thinking he had actually given the commission of writing this new book a negative meaning which seemingly prompted his writer's block.

All of us have jobs which we have not got round to doing.

More often than not, despite the many lame excuses for inactivity that we come up with, the real reason is that the activity has no perceived clear or valued meaning for us. The challenge for the successful seed of recovery is to create positive meaning for any task.

During a creativity training course for a group of radio advertising creatives, one delegate recalled how he struggled to come up with ideas for a campaign to recruit Special Constables (unpaid volunteer police officers.)

The guy remembered the thought process going through his head: *'Why would anyone want to be an unpaid copper?'* He had successfully created for himself negative meaning to the assignment – which provided a barrier for his normal creative flow.

He could have reframed the brief in a beautiful question, identifying a value which had personal meaning to him, such as: *'I want to live in a community where people can feel safe'*. He then could have gone more easily about his task of generating ideas to address this challenge.

You have got to keep at it if your green shoot is to flourish.

There's no such thing as a guaranteed winning lottery ticket.

Persistence usually pays (except for lottery tickets!). Every time you do something you learn from it and have the opportunity to find a way to do it better next time.

The old golfing cliché 'the harder you prepare the luckier you seem to get' is as true in life as it is on the golf course.

Successful green shoots combine the ability to take risks but also to stick with things. They have the talent to know when to drop something and walk away. The more options and opportunities you have the more flexibility you have at your disposal.

Your Adversity Quotient skills enable you to respond positively to changes or setbacks where you remain calm and in control of your emotions. You manage pressure well, working productively in challenging situations by keeping your emotions under control and remaining emotionally stable.

'Doing' gets you more than 'saying' is so true. There will be many times when you will need to be tough to deliver what you believe to be right.

I was fortunate in gaining from the experience of helping to bring up my younger brother Kevin. Kevin was born autistic with a range of severe behavioural problems.

Now, as a child taking my kid brother out on the streets of the East End of London I used to see out of the corner of my eye, people looking at us, even making fun of us behind our backs as a result of Kevin's 'unorthodox' behaviour.

These experiences may have hurt at the time. But they also helped harden me up, making me mentally tougher as a person. It helped me to better respond to future challenges by boosting my Adversity Quotient, to bounce back from any setbacks. In fact I liken disability to being a celebrity – you get noticed everywhere. Disability just lacks the fame and fortune.

When I share Kevin's story with people I invariably get people relating their own similar stories, when life hasn't been good. Similarly, they reflect how they too have grown from the experience and are able to face what life throws at them next.

In being a seed for a green shoot you need to expect disappointment, setbacks, people saying 'No' and even slamming the door in your face or putting the phone down on you.

Like the characters in *'Rocky'* and *'The Shawshank Redemption'* you can choose to stay down when knocked down, or you can choose to bounce back.

You cannot buy an insurance policy against all problems. But, by harnessing your Adversity Quotient, it can serve as your rocket fuel to help you bounce back. Expect future obstacles and difficulties but aim to meet problems and obstacles as they arise.

We all have the equivalent of a medal case, with individual medals earned from different situations when we have had to stand up and be counted or go the extra yard in some way. These achievements are real, and have deep meaning for you.

This is truly an asset and is not to be left gathering dust in your equivalent of a medal case. Instead, their memory and inspiration can be invoked whenever you feel your green shoot is not growing, when someone else is trampling it down, when you are being thwarted in some way. Use it whenever your green shoot meets an obstacle.

Each of us has the equivalent of a medal collection of experiences.

Draw upon these experiences and create new medals to add to your collection as you overcome the challenges and obstacles in your way of becoming a green shoot.

Your green shoot Action Steps

1. *Think back to a time when you have been magnificent or even ever so slightly magnificent. How would the magnificent you respond differently to challenges you are facing now?*

2. *What ways can you be an inspirational, positive role model for yourself or others?*

3. *What meaning can you identify or inject into your challenge to be a green shoot?*

4. *What new medals can you add to your medal case when you have been positive, strong, assertive, or bounced back in some way during the last 24 hours?*

5. *Can you have another go at something you have given up on or not fully exploited?*

13. Beautiful boxes for your thinking (and how to work even in your sleep)

The nub to outstanding creative thinking is not about coming up with a 1001½ different ideas.

It's actually about making sure you ask the right question, what I call 'the beautiful question'. Whenever you are faced with a problem you immediately frame it as a question: 'How can I....?'

Posing a question is the first step in being creative, in coming up with a different way of tackling your reality. The beautiful question enables you to get at the heart of any issue, any challenge you face. I actually define 'creativity' as:

> *'Flexible thinking around beautiful questions*
> *in your quest to add value'.*

You can tell when you have a beautiful question because it makes the solutions flow easily from your mind. In fact, you ooze ideas when you have the right question.

You have probably heard of the phrase 'outside the box thinking' to describe novel, unusual, far out, right-field, maybe wacky solutions. The phrase pre-supposes there is a box that contains the existing thoughts and solutions, and the new outside the box idea comes from outside the territory to redefine the situation.

I would suggest there is no such thing as 'outside the box' thinking.

All ideas exist within boxes. The posh word for these boxes is a 'paradigm' or 'frame'. We see the world through our own unique picture frame. This 'picture frame' is the box of our thinking: it captures a scene in all senses of the word, by providing you with a range of vision for the task before you. It also defines your world by excluding things beyond its boundaries.

This picture frame is your paradigm. If you look in the dictionary the word 'paradigm' tends to refer to a general mindset. I prefer to define it as the boundary of your perception. (The word 'paradigm' has been out of favour in management-speak, people fearing it has become a cliché, an easy term to parody. I don't care about this, and still prefer to use it, as it is more specific and helpful than the alternative word 'frame'.)

Creativity is about managed incongruity. You have a choice of how you manage and manipulate the box of your thinking. The box acts as a tool to help you manage your world as you see it before you. It also acts as a prison cell in restricting what you perceive before you.

Think for a moment. Which of the words below is the odd one out?

carrot, onion, parsnip, pear, potato

The obvious answer it would seem is 'pear', the only fruit, because all the other words are vegetables.

Yet, you could have chosen 'onion' because it is the only word beginning with a vowel.

What you have demonstrated is how when faced with any new information or problem your mind jumps to conclusions about how the different bits of data relate to each other, and what you know already, and selects what you regard as the 'obvious'.

Invariably, there is always more than one answer. Different answers might be better in different situations.

So, in effect your mind has created a box - a bit like a picture frame - to enable you to understand, make sense, manage what you have before you, in order to help you see a coherent picture.

Many of us are engaged in what I call 'same box' thinking: operating within the same boundaries, doing the same thing, and wishfully hoping to get the same results. As a strategy during the age of disruption, this type of thinking is not going to get you far. It will in fact leave you further behind your world.

We 'do not see' even evidence that does not fit our current paradigm. We can suffer from 'truthiness' a word coined by American comedian Stephen Colbert as the quality of preferring concepts or facts one wishes to be true, rather than concepts or facts known to be true.

Your paradigm, the picture frame on any problem you have is actually made up of assumptions – even assumptions you merely wish to be true. Because you are surrounded by a world of infinite complexity you will make certain assumptions to simplify problems and to make them less complex and easier to handle.

This is best illustrated by the apocryphal story about the artist Picasso. While on a train journey he was spotted by someone who remonstrated: *"Why couldn't he paint more life-like pictures?"*

When Picasso asked what was meant by 'life-like' the gentleman produced a photograph of his wife from his wallet. Picasso replied by saying how small and flat she was.

The man assumed the photograph was life-like. Picasso challenged his assumptions.

The most powerful creativity tool I share in my training courses is a simple question: *"What assumptions am I making?"*

It is a seemingly obvious, common sense question. But like the old adage, what is often common is not sensible, and what is sensible is not often common.

By posing this question it helps to dismantle, to unravel the picture frame of your landscape, to allow in new possibilities, or details which you may have previously overlooked.

So with any situation you have a ready range of beautiful questions including:

"What assumptions am I making?"

"What Red Light Thinking do I need to do? (i.e. is there new information you can find out, what will be the logical steps of this situation.)

"How can I Big Box this?" - what bigger context is there to your situation

"How can I small Box this?" – what detail within my situation can I make more of.

"How can I different box this?" – where else can I start to look at my situation from, in order to generate new

insights, perspectives and new solutions.

"Where's the added value of any new ideas?"

'Bigger Box Thinking' is where you redefine the boundaries of your 'picture frame' to expand your range of available options. The ability to identify more opportunities than the expected, than others are seeing, will obviously help you in responding to the age of disruption.

Small Box Thinking can help break down the detail of your situation. By changing different parts within your established landscape you can create significant added value. This gives you the potential to spot differences, new things, which others may overlook.

Lastly, you have the choice of Different Box Thinking; by starting from somewhere different you will see your world differently. Most creativity techniques are based on Different Box Thinking, to provide a new spark, a new way of looking at your problem.

In the age of disruption there are three big strategic questions you need to consider.

Imagine there are three pots; one is empty, the second contains positive opportunities actually created by the downturn, and the third has new things, stuff not yet invented, or things with the potential to be made more widely available.

Which of these three pots should you dip into in order to create your future green shoot?

Being creative and resourceful is not about being a super being creating miracles, results from the hardest of challenges. If you go to the cupboard and the cupboard is bare, you are best off going to a different cupboard. In your work, if you are doing a job where the market has dried up, the most beautiful question you could pose yourself is:

"Am I better looking in the other pots of who does well in a recession or who is offering a new thing?"

It is a bit like the story of the tourist in Ireland who was told when asking for directions: *"If I was you, I wouldn't be starting from here."*

In facing the downturn and needing to be a green shoot, you need to use your pit stop pessimism and face up to, and address the fundamental question of where is the best place to start then considering if you would be better starting from somewhere else.

Again, one positive from the downturn is that it is forcing people to make decisions because they have been forced into a new situation.

Your beautiful questions exist on a number of different levels - objective, strategic and tactical.

People often confuse these different levels. Maybe it can be best explained by an analogy; if the objective is to get drunk, a strategy could be to go to the pub, and the tactics are to drink ten pints.

I believe the word 'strategy' is over-used. When people say they need a strategy report, it is often used because they have no idea what they actually need or want. They should instead say, *"We need an objectives report"*.

People have a more professional attitude to going on a diet, than they do when trying to make a difference in other parts of their lives. The first thing you do when dieting is to weigh yourself, giving you a measure of where you are now. You then choose a target weight which provides a goal for your efforts, as well as enabling you to assess how successful you have been.

What is the equivalent of the weighing scales in your task to become a new green shoot?

Some beautiful questions to consider when looking in the pot of 'who does well in a recession' include:

- Which markets grow in a downturn?
- What downturn needs are there which need to be met?
- What are people substituting in their lives - what are they now using instead of what they used before?
- What is an affordable luxury in the downturn? (Even when consumers cut back they still enjoy products that can give pleasure, entertainment or even a distraction from difficult times around them.)
- Which products or services deliver value for money when consumer budgets are tight?

Some beautiful questions to ask when looking in the pot of new things include:

- What new needs do people have because they have more enforced free time?
- What niggles me? Can I provide a solution to this?
- Where are there going to be two people passing money to each other, and how can I get in between them?

Your most powerful creative thinking technique is not a brainstorm or some clever computer software. It is your brain when it is asleep.

You will get your best quality, most powerful ideas from your incubation – when you sleep on a problem and let your unconscious mind get to grips with it.

The problem with incubation however, is getting it to work to order. I have tried it with my clients, telling them *"I'm incubating"* and they won't let me get away with it.

Beautiful questions are your best fishing line for incubation. By posing your beautiful questions and sleeping on them, you are harnessing a fuller capacity of the brain and able to hook previously elusive ideas.

Imagine your brain is a big factory, with a massive production floor and a tiny room with just a few bits of equipment. Well, in life's daily grind we tend to spend most of our time on the immediate, the now, the instant. As a result we primarily operate from within the small room, with its limited capacity.

The small room represents our conscious brain and the factory floor is what we could call our unconscious. By posing a question and then getting on with something else we are priming our brains to consider more fully, to explore new dimensions, and to make greater use of its capabilities. In this way , it creates the potential to later come up, often quite out of the blue with a powerful new insight or solution to your challenge.

A tip you can use to help manage your incubation is to tightly define your question. Again, you can use beautiful questions to help you precisely define your situation:

- What is the equivalent of the dieter's weighing scales which could give you a measure of where you are at now?
- What will your success look and feel like – and what do you need to do to make that happen?
- What precisely are you after, what are you wanting to achieve?
- How will you feel if you do nothing?
- What are the benefits or disadvantages of doing nothing?

By using tighter, more precisely defined questions, the more likely your subsequent flashes of inspiration will be relevant to your challenge.

Use incubation at every opportunity: when you go to sleep, during a coffee or lunch break, in that trip to the bathroom, even while walking to the door and back of the room you are in - all provide incubation breaks. (Why not take an incubation break now to think about how to create more incubation time?)

The worrying trend in modern-day life is how our incubation time is being squeezed. How often are you using your mobile phone when walking, or checking your e mails while talking to someone on the phone? These all act as constraints, dampeners on your incubation, squeezing out time for your mind to roam and think freely.

When you do come up with ideas – or illuminations as I call them, remember to make a note of them. These illuminations are your unconscious talking to you. Often these ideas will not be concrete, ready-made solutions. But rather they will be stepping stones to take you down the path to a solution.

Using beautiful boxes to frame your questions and flexibly thinking between Big, Small and Different boxes will enable you to think more flexibly than anyone in same box thinking mode. And you can even do it while you are asleep.

Beautiful questions are at the heart of your ability to come up with new ideas, overcome problems, redefine your reality in some way – and define the box of your thinking.

Challenge your assumptions, challenge the thinking of others, or the world at large through your beautiful questions. By recognising you have different levels of Big, Small and Different box thinking you can help yourself to think more flexibly. It will enable your green shoot to grow and overcome the obstacles holding back others who are just thinking in one dimension.

Your green shoot Action Steps

1. *Ask, what assumptions are you making, or the wider world is making?*

2. *Examining your situation, how can you use Big Box (think about in a wider, larger context), or Small Box (think about a detail of your reality), or Different Box Thinking (start your thinking from a different place)?*

3. *What questions should you be asking yourself before you go to sleep?*

4. *Assessing your current situation what is the equivalent of 'the empty pot', the 'pot of who does well in a recession' and the 'pot of new things'?*

5. *What assumptions are you making about your assumptions?*

14. Your Martini clock - opportunities any time, any place, any where,

We are all time travellers – it's just that most of us travel at one speed, in one direction and use just one gear.

The time you have taken to read this sentence marks a journey of one or two seconds through time. That may not have been one of your life's most exciting experiences. But just imagine if you were able to travel faster through time, and backwards and forwards. What a competitive advantage it would give you for spotting what people want, the equivalent of what horses to back, what pitfalls to avoid, as well as picking up great lessons from heroes past and future.

In my talks I sometimes hold up a copy of the 'Financial Times'. In 2009 it retails in the UK for £2 a copy. I ask the audience how much would they pay for yesterdays or the day before, or a year old copy. I don't get many takers for old news. In fact the newspaper acquires a negative value for me, as in my office, I pay for our paper to be recycled.

Yet, what if I was to offer for sale a copy of tomorrow's 'Financial Times', or next year's, or the year after that, or one from 2020? How much would people pay me?

I get lots of potential bidders for the newspaper of the future. (Except for one guy who told me he would not be interested, as there are no racing results in the FT!)

I am going to make a self-limiting statement here; I cannot alter the rules of quantum physics: I cannot physically take you back or forwards in time.

What I can do is help you be more a more flexible time traveller to spot the opportunities one-dimensional people will miss. Your flexible thinking will enable you to more effectively reach out in the future, the past, and the present.

The science fiction writer William Gibson gave the world the phrase, *"the future is already here. It is just unevenly distributed."*

What he means is that new things or inventions are like famous people of achievement; they don't necessarily get noticed when they are born.

New things in the year 2020 which will appear different, strange or unusual to us now will have their seeds, roots and shoots in the present.

I was around in 1972 but don't remember the Internet then. And yet it was invented then. Neither, as a child, do I recall mobile phones or Tandoori Chicken Masala; but they were also invented in the 1970's.

The events of 9/11 are recognised as a major landmark in the 21st century. The idea of an attack by terrorists on major iconic landmarks was a shock, a surprise, just unthinkable.

Shame no one listened to France's best-known, anti-terrorist judge, Jean-Louis Brugiere. As a *'Financial Times'* journalist noted in a 2005 interview: *"Mr. Brugiere has been warning about the risk of terrorists using an aircraft as a bomb after foiling the 1994 hijacking of an Air France jet by Algerian radicals planning to crash it into the Eiffel tower. People pay more attention to him now."*

Even the most unthinkable things somehow present clues, some evidence which the sagacious opportunity spotter can detect to seize an advantage over other time travellers.

How much of a surprise was the global downturn or the credit crunch, particularly those familiar with episodes such as the Tulip Mania of 1637 , or other such examples of financial speculations?

To be a green shoot in the Upturn, you may not be able to do much about quantum physics but your flexible mind can scope, search out and succeed in finding new opportunities which others will miss.

As an opportunity hunter you will need what I call a 'Martini clock' – because ideas come, like the ad says, anytime, anyplace, anywhere. Opportunity hunters should never clock off. Opportunities are 24 7.

I believe you are never more than 12 feet from an opportunity. During a tour of Australia I was working with a group of college staff. I started the session, pen at the ready in front of my flip chart and asked the delegates what they wanted to learn from the day. Some smart-arsed woman shouted out: *I want to learn to play the guitar!*" Luckily for me, a guy on the next table offered to teach her.

This served as a wonderful demonstration of how anyone within 12 feet of you represents a potential solution to any problem you have; they might know an answer, or know someone who can help.

I chose 12 feet, as in one week I came across two

statistics: in a building you are never more than 12 feet away from an electric motor, or a rat! (I have since also discovered, you are never more than 12ft from a Manchester United supporter at any public event.)

Any object within 12 feet of you represents a design solution to a problem which can offer a direct idea to use in your situation, or trigger a line of thought or inspiration to help you arrive at a solution.

Your ability to best read the future from the present – the equivalent of having a newspaper from the future – is called your sagacity.

We all have brilliant 20:20 vision for spotting opportunities. We can clearly see the chances waiting to be taken, and how, if developed, they would make your future better in some way.

This vision for many people is frustratingly limited to the past. By looking back at our own history, we can see now, in crystal clarity, what we may have missed at the time.

This 20:20 vision is called hindsight.

I would define sagacity as seeing now, what you would see in hindsight.

Your sagacity is like an opportunity spotting radar - able to detect things out there beyond you, and give you an advance warning of their arrival.

The great news is that we all have a sagacity muscle within us, and like any muscle, the more you focus and exercise it, the better it will become, giving you a better chance of 20:20 vision.

The first change is to believe there are opportunities. I tell the story of my wife when she goes into the store TK Maxx. There are two schools of thought about this store. One group describing the rows of often untidy racks and shelves says: 'You can never find what you want in there, it's like a jumble sale' My wife however, says she always comes out with a bargain. She always goes in with a shopping trolley.

Who is more likely to find a bargain, the person who says 'You can never find what you want in there', or the person with the shopping trolley?

Are you going to go through life saying you don't have any luck and can't find what you want? Or are you living your life with a metaphorical shopping trolley at hand, to pick up the bargains of opportunity within 12 foot of you.

Because of our expanding world knowledge, we need to similarly expand our vocabulary. To give ourselves new tools to better manage our new universe, I coined the term 'Hibris'. It describes how we need to have a sense of arrogance about our own ability to succeed and find opportunities, tempered with a humility to recognise we do not know everything, how it is important to listen and learn, even from the most unlikely of sources.

One of the challenges facing the opportunity hunter is how many potentially great ideas are hidden, camouflaged amidst the noise of confusing detail. You need to have a hibris attitude state to succeed.

An example of this was my campaign to save the 'wobble' on London's Millennium footbridge.

Back in June 2000 the Millennium footbridge was closed within three days of its opening because it had a 'wobble'; when large numbers of visitors walked across they could sense a movement, the 'wobble'.

They were not in danger of being plunged into the river Thames, but the wobble was not part of the specification, it was an unforeseen glitch. Like any glitch it simply had to be removed.

A year later, costing some £5 million as well as much embarrassment to the reputation of British engineering and design, the bridge was de-wobbled (or some other engineering term) and re-opened.

Yet, was the wobble a problem?

Let's be time travellers to the past; it's called doing research and using your imagination.

Let's go back to the year 1173, to an unremarkable northern Italian city. Imagine you are in the Mayor's office and through one door a panic-stricken Chief Engineer come in and screams: *"Our new campanile has developed a lean! We will have to spend 5 million lire to put it straight!"* through the other door comes the Head of Tourism who offers an alternative strategy: *"There might be something in this. We should keep the lean."*

If you are the Mayor who should you listen to?

Who did we in Britain listen to?

During 2008 Pisa and its leaning tower received over 2.6 million visitors. Just as well they didn't listen to their engineering chief.

If you use your flexible thinking boxes to examine the situation - some bigger box thinking – it can put your reality into a bigger context, just as travelling back in time would do to reveal new insights.

In one box the Millennium footbridge has to get you across from one side of the river to the other without your feet getting wet.

It sits within a bigger box of getting you across with a degree of safety and comfort – you wouldn't want a rope bridge across the river Thames in the middle of London.

Within an even bigger box - the bridge also exists as a tourist attraction.

Instead of the wobble being a problem it could, and should have been seen as an opportunity, albeit an uninvited and unexpected guest.

Because it wasn't part of a pre-planned script, its intrusion was seen in the negative. (Particularly, as it did, coming at a politically sensitive time when the Millennium dome was being heavily criticised.) Anything not going to plan was therefore seen as subversive, undesirable, and needed eliminating.

It saddens me that the opportunity of the wobble was not realised.

But as a story it does capture the challenge faced by the

opportunity hunter.

Firstly, opportunities don't come gift-wrapped, clearly announcing what they are, and their potential. They are often ambiguous, camouflaged, half-hidden, inverted, adopting disguises that have successfully deflected everyone else – except you.

Secondly, if you have an idea, one that goes against the grain, swims against the tide of prevailing thought and orthodoxy, you will most likely not get instant recognition, or be lauded as the new Messiah. Instead, you may face ridicule or be ignored.

My campaign to save the wobble was met with derision. And was ignored by the decision makers. I take great comfort from the words of the musician Frank Zappa when he said: *"Just because several million people think you're wrong doesn't mean they're right."*

I have also created another term 'Ideapoo'. You need to recognise that in your journey to spot opportunities, many ideas need to be shaped or carved out, nurtured and grown before they can offer you a realizable asset. You need to develop a tolerance of 'Ideapoo', the numerous, poor quality, poo ideas you need to wade through, and live with, before your gem of an idea emerges.

Big enemies to your opportunity cultivation are premature evaluation, where you are judgmental too soon, and premature consolidation, where you stop exploring new options and just build up from where you are at.

I like the story attributed to Einstein that he was once asked what the difference between himself and the average person was. He replied that the average person if looking for a needle in a haystack would stop when they found a needle. He, however, would tear through the entire haystack looking for all possible needles.

I often find people blind themselves to potentially good ideas by being reluctant to play with loose concepts, to get their hands dirty exploring raw ideas. They have a set view that an idea must be ready to run, be set in concrete detail; otherwise they will not entertain it as a valid concept.

Even the most phenomenal of ideas sound stupid when explained in their bald facts. (Have you ever tried explaining the facts of life to a child?)

If you were to put a seed on a pedestal it actually prevents it from gaining nourishment from its immediate environment and growing. Ultimately, without such growth it will shrivel away and die.

The same applies to your ideas for being a green shoot. You don't just need to spot an idea, but also need to ensure it can grow and develop and fulfil its potential.

You need to be able to tolerate ambiguity, a possible lack of clarity in what faces you.

The great news is that we all have some sagacity. We all have what I call 'small box sagacity' based around our professional expertise or a special interest.

Our detailed specific knowledge will enable you to spot

things others will miss. I have a builder friend and he will spot things about the room he enters which I would be oblivious too because of his trade knowledge. Yet, given my working life in the media communications world, I will spot things about a media story he would miss, because of my specialist knowledge.

To boost your big box sagacity – your skill in seeing your world in a bigger context - you need to start looking at the world in a different way. You need to apply the excited anticipation of an adventurer in an exotic land to your own backyard.

By detaching yourself from the familiar, you will spot things which others around you will miss.

A sense crucial in spotting opportunities are your listening skills. I always think that big people monopolize listening, small people monopolize talking. Your ears will never get you into trouble and are crucial antennae for picking up new things. Coupled with a genuine desire to respect and value the other person's view, you will hear far more than the self-centred person who just talks about them, and only them.

Another great seedbed for opportunities are setbacks, operational inexactitudes – cock-ups, and negative news.

I had a chance encounter with the former Prime Minster Tony Blair, and basically I fluffed the opportunity to say anything meaningful. Relating the tale to a publisher friend, we then created the idea of a new book, *'A Minute with Tony Blair'*. In one minute the average person can say about 150 words (170 words in my case.)

We then invited a range of celebrities and a cross section of the community to provide their response to the question: *'If you had a minute with Tony Blair, what would you say?'*

The result was a great little book, providing a platform for a variety of pertinent, and sometimes flippant comments, some money raised for Amnesty International, and some great media moments on BBC Radio 4 and in national media for yours truly.

And it all came about from regretting a missed opportunity. Rather than moping about it, it was instead turned into a positive opportunity.

One person's downturn is another's up-opportunity. The collapse of the dot com bubble for example, has led to the rise of a host of new applications collectively know as Web 2.0 technologies.

The lesson for you is to ask in what ways can you flexibly turn any negative into a positive, or identify a seed of new opportunity within the gloom?

There will no doubt be more opportunities for providing services for people on low incomes, in data protection, fighting climate change, from diminishing public sector budgets - anything you see in the media as a problem provides opportunities for someone who can come up with a solution, or even part of a solution.

A key characteristic of the flexible thinker is that they keep being switched on, when others switch off. Opportunity hunting is 24 7.

To become a green shoot, be like a Martini clock
–opportunities are there for you,

    any time,

    any place,

    any where.

Your green shoot Action Steps

1. *Explore the area 12 ft around you; the people, the objects, the inter-relationships, or different combinations within this space. How can they be used as solutions, inspirations in your thinking about being a green shoot?*

2. *Looking back on your life, what opportunities have you, in hindsight, missed out on? Imagine that you of the future can advise you now on what you should do. What advice are you likely to be given?*

3. *What negatives, cock-ups, problems can you turn around into opportunities for you?*

4. *Imagine you have a shopping trolley going through life picking up available opportunities, half-opportunities, or even vague notions of ideas which could help you. What sort of things would you be putting into your trolley to help you be a successful green shoot?*

5. *What extra thing could you be doing to become a green shoot?*

A cocktail of flexibility - Leaving Section II and entering Section III

You have read about your different skills, or thinking quotients, which provide the source for your resourcefulness.

Any situation you face will require a different recipe, a blend of different resources to meet the specific needs of the hour.

Sometimes you need to be resolute, tough, determined to succeed. This is where you draw upon your Adversity Quotient.

Other times you need to look ahead, stand away from your immediate worries, realities and visit the future by creating your Big Bungee Vision and use you Vision Quotient.

There will be problems ahead when you need to think through the worst scenarios using your Red Light Thinking where you engage your Intelligence Quotient. Alternatively, you may need to wed yourself to the positive, using your Green Light Thinking and your Emotional Quotient skills.

Other challenges will require detail, analysis and asking beautiful questions, or you may need to dream, create new, unfounded, unproven but real to you solutions.

No two situations are the same.

I am reminded of the power of context whilst at a comedy gig starring Ken Dodd. An element of Ken's act consists of picking on the audience. He picked on me. *"You Sir, what's your surname?"* *"Green"* I replied. *"Do you know that means handsome, strong, gentle and kind."* Before I could get too big headed he then asked: *"What's your first name?"* I shouted back *"Andy"*, and quick as a flash he said: *"That means not very."*

To cope with, or succeed in the age of disruption, you need to be flexible. The greater understanding you now have of your different quotients enables you to draw upon them whenever necessary and provide you with a wider range of responses.

In the age of disruption however, you will need to think flexibly, but also to think flexibly faster. Section III provides you with a range of tools to speed up your resourcefulness in order to make you more Golden Swan friendly.

15. Be an opportunity magnet

In the age of disruption it's not just about thinking more flexibly to maximise your response to the changing world around you. You need to think flexibly faster.

If you want to gain a competitive edge, to reap the full dividends of whatever opportunity you are creating, you have got to bring your idea quicker to market. In the Internet age your competitor is not just down the road; they are at a keyboard or Blackberry anywhere in the world.

You need to think differently to create your seed of opportunity. Yet, your seed will remain a seed if you are slow to think, respond and act differently.

To become a green shoot you need to be more opportunistic and faster.

It is curious that if you describe someone as an 'opportunist' it is often said in a derogatory context, and is usually meant as an insult.

Somehow, someone who is able to be pragmatic, to read the situation they face, and take advantage of available opportunities is seen in the negative.

This paradox might be down to the feeling if someone jumps at an opportunity, they may be deemed to unprincipled, lacking in substance. They simply can't be trusted.

The irony is that to be an outstanding opportunist you actually need to be strongly principled. You need a strong sense of who you are, what you stand for, and where you are going with your life.

By having this strong sense of purpose it acts as an opportunity magnet. Things start coming to you. You make yourself more attractive to other people's generosity, which becomes your luck.

So, what can you do to enhance yourself as an opportunity magnet?

In essence you need to do five things:

- Know what you want and have some sense of where you want to be
- Recognise you are a 'brand' and manage your brand.
- Live by example
- Create memorable, 'sticky' messages about yourself
- Connect with other people and build your networks

These actions are collectively called 'personal brandcasting'.

People often think the word 'brand' is just for consumer products like Coca Cola, Virgin, or Levis. The concept however, is relevant to you, me and everyone else you know.

You don't have the choice to be a brand or not. You have a choice to manage your brand. For many, their personal brands are ill-defined, fuzzy or incoherent. This hampers their ability to respond to opportunities and think flexibly faster. As a result they make themselves poor, often lousy, opportunity magnets.

If you want to think flexibly faster, you need to manage your brand, define who you are, help people remember you more easily, and ensure they know what your quest is, and what you are after.

People come in all shapes and sizes. Outstanding opportunists work from having a strong self brand.

Your brand is made up of three elements:

- Your icons – what do people instantly remember you by.
-
- Your values – what is important to you and determines what you prioritise and do.
-
- Your information – what are your sexy, sticky, killer facts that describe you and your quest.

It is possible to manage your brand and reputation by addressing each of these three areas.

If I was to say to you the words 'New York City' what images do you see in your mind? Some may say a famous landmark, such as the Empire State building, the Statue of Liberty, the Twin Towers. Others might say a famous person, objects such as Yellow taxi cabs, pastrami sandwiches or other food, or a logo.

There is no right or answer. It demonstrates that 'New York City' is an icon rich brand. It is able to generate many different instant mental pictures.

If I was to give you another place name, such as Wakefield in West Yorkshire, unless you are from the area, you are unlikely to have a strong mental picture. Wakefield in contrast, is a relatively icon-poor brand.

People often confuse the word 'brand' with a logo, a graphic badge that people feel is the sum of what is meant by 'brand'. Yet two of the world's most famous brands don't have a logo: have you seen a logo for the Mafia, or Al-Quaida?

They are both brands, yet neither has an official logo. So, it's possible to have brands without a logo. A logo is not fundamental to your brand.

The crucial element is to have icons, pictures which are generated in people's minds when your name is mentioned.

You will have created icons through contact with others: the way you look, speak, treat people, act and behave. So, for example, when people meet me, they say 'he's that big guy, from London'. (If you don't know me, I am now helping to create a picture in your mind with just a few sentences.)

Every way you turn you will have potential icons: your work – you might be known as the accountant, the plumber, the doctor, or the teacher, whatever your job is. Or it might be your family, where you are known by others as the partner of, or cousin of, parent of and so on.

You will have icons through you what you do: you are the person who is known to have written that book, or stopped the traffic the time....

You will have icons with your associations – you are the person who worked at, or provided a service to so and so, or supports a certain football team. (I'm West Ham United by the way.)

You will have icons with your past, and your future – you are the person who used to, or is going to, do certain things.

All these things around you can either be iconic – in that you are already known by them, or seed icons, where with a bit of management and cultivation on your part you can create potential instant mental images whenever your name is mentioned.

Most of us, simply avoid actively managing how we want other people to see us. We make decisions at an unconscious level, just getting on with life, adopting things we like, feel comfortable with, or want to conform to, so we can be part of the crowd, (or becoming invisible within the crowd).

We can fail to help ourselves by not managing our brand icons. We expect others to know us, and crucially, know where we are going. You need to ask yourself what can you do to make people remember you more? What can you do to get people to take your call, open their doors to you, and let you through quicker?

When making yourself memorable you need to ensure you are offering people appropriate cues and clues to who you are.

I remember a business networking event where everyone had to introduce themselves. One guy stood up and had a purple toy donkey on his arm. He announced: *"You are probably wondering why I have this donkey? It's so that you can remember me!"* My thoughts were unflattering on how people will remember him, for the wrong reasons.

It is important that whatever you choose to do or say about yourself is credible and has integrity with you, your mission, and what you stand for. Your messages should also contain a 'What's-In-It-For-Me benefit' – what is it you can offer to make the other person's world better?

One way of finding out about yourself is asking others for five words or things that describe you – the more you ask, the more you will get an understanding of your wider currency.

Another valuable tool for knowing yourself - your intra personal knowledge - is to identify your values; what is it that is important to you, which determines what you do, and don't do. I would recommend identifying your five key values and establishing the order of priority they take. The trick is to identify what you tend to do first, as this reveals where your real priorities lie.

As a values specialist Jackie Le Fevre suggests, values are the energy that provides you with your own unique internal engine to keep you going, even when the odds are stacked against you.

Our values help us shape how we respond to different experiences. As a budding green shoot, you need to ask yourself what values you need to underpin your actions in order be successful.

By consciously choosing new values, and regularly reaffirming them to yourself, you can consciously harness values that will nurture your green shoot.

The third element of your brand, alongside icons and values is the facts and details about you – your information. Here you need to identify what key sexy facts you need to use to describe yourself. The facts that capture what your goals are, what opportunities you are seeking to help you achieve these goals, and how others can help you in your quest.

In a business context for example, I tell people whom I meet for the first time:

> *"My name is Andy Green. I help improve my clients' ability to think more flexibly and creatively so they can achieve more with less. I do this through running training sessions or team awaydays, and speaking at conferences."*

I also make it easy for them to find out that I have written several books on creative thinking and that I travel around the world sharing my expertise. This provides legitimacy to my claims.

As a result, they know what I do for other people, and could potentially for them, and also how I do it, and what sort of things I need to help me in my quest

The most profound element in how you communicate is to lead by example: what you do is more important than what you say. You can lead and inspire others by your actions.

Aligning your brand with your mission in life helps provide nourishment to your ethical passion, enabling you to recognise quicker what is the right thing to do in any situation.

Another great tool in deciding what is the right thing to do in any complex situation, is to use role models – people, alive or dead, fact or fiction, famous or familiar, who inspire you in some way.

A frequent role model I use is the fictional character of the Lieutenant in the film *'Saving Private Ryan'*.

He strikes me as an intelligent, thoughtful person who seems to share similar values to me. In my mind I ask the questions: 'What would he do in this situation I face?' 'What would he think is the right thing to do here?'

I would recommend having a wardrobe of role models – to suit different needs and occasions – which will provide a very powerful asset in becoming a green shoot.

Having a clarity of thought - prompted by the role model - about what is the right thing for you, gives you more energy by creating focus for your efforts and provides immense power to your actions and your communications.

You have limited resources. You may not have much, or any money. In the age of disruption you need to respond to the world quicker, and also get the world to respond quicker to you.

Having this clarity around your brand makes it easier for people to remember you, and what you are doing with your life. It helps bring you front of mind with reference to specific opportunities they may have.

A further dimension in being an opportunity magnet is to have a team working for you. There is only one of you, so the more hands you can have to help you, extends your reach, enables you to be almost in two places at once and gets you into places you would not necessarily dream of getting into.

The idea of a team working for you is a proven communications model. Teams of twelve seem an optimum number for spreading your word, looking out for opportunities, and making connections for you, enabling you to achieve great changes in your world.

Without appearing flippant or disrespectful, these are your 'disciples', your 'connectors'.

A man, some 2,000 years ago, had no money, yet had an immensely strong, powerful personal brand and the help of twelve people to spread his message.

Did Jesus Christ have the services of Saatchi & Saatchi Bethlehem branch and pots of cash to create a worldwide religion? (You can actually use any major religious figure to make this point.) But he did have an immensely strong personal brand, he lived by example, created sticky messages – or parables about himself – and had his team of disciples.

Your disciples, or connectors, are people who make things happen for you. They can recommend you to other people. They can alert you to new opportunities or useful bits of information.

Yet, why should someone else give up their valuable time and energy and most importantly, put their credibility on the line for you?

The answer is that you have built up respect, trust, and commitment with them. It is human nature to reciprocate when you feel you owe someone, when someone has done something for you.

The biggest mistake people make when business networking is expecting just to take; they want others to give to them.

What they should instead be doing is seeking to give; what can they offer to someone else that will be useful, valued and make a difference to the other person's life.

By giving, you are investing in a relationship. It is laying down the seeds of cultivating a potential connector who one day may help you.

Besides, giving is a much more gratifying aspect of life than taking. It makes you feel better about yourself. It provides proof that you are indeed, a wonderful human being.

In managing your relationship with your connectors you need to be responsive to their needs. No, let's re-phrase that; you need to be ultra-responsive. When they say 'jump', you jump even higher.

While on a family holiday in Siena, Italy, my mobile phone rang. It was one of my connectors needing help. I didn't tell them to *"Go away, I'm on holiday."* Instead, I acted immediately. It was a problem for which I couldn't provide the right answer, but I knew a person who could.

Five minutes and two phone calls later, I had a happy connector.

Sure, I had to briefly compromise my interests of being on holiday. But I don't let my connectors down. It was largely down to them that I could afford the holiday in the first place.

I find that when I am not enjoying the business success I should, I need to re-examine my connectors; what have I done for them lately? Do I need recruit new connectors? Your success in life is down to the quality of your connectors.

When I counsel individuals about managing their connector relationships, I typically find most usually have just three or four connectors in their life. My target is 12. It is big enough to offer a diverse front, and widely reach out to the outside world. Yet, it is sufficiently small enough to adequately manage, service and ensure you make a difference to their life.

By managing your personal brandcasting – your brand, your actions, your sticky messages and your networks - other people will have a clear idea of who you are, what you stand for, where you are going with your life.

They will positively feel pre-disposed to you, possibly as a result of you having given them something, or having cultivated their relationship.

All this adds up to your being a more powerful opportunity magnet; the more things that come your way, the more options you have to flexibly adapt and create new opportunities for your green shoot.

It helps you think flexibly faster.

Your green shoot Action Steps

1. *What is your mission in being a green shoot? What do you want to achieve? What do you need from others and the outside world to achieve this?*

2. *What do you stand for – and against?*

3. *What ways can you improve your 'personal brandcasting' – who you are in terms of your brand, how you communicate this brand through your actions, how you help others to spread your word by creating word of mouth friendly messages about yourself which are memorable and easily pass-onable, and how you cultivate networks of friends, supporters and connectors to make things happen for you?*

4. *What are your personal brand icons, values and sexy facts about you and the green shoot you are creating?*

5. *Who are your connectors – can you identify new members for your team of disciples – and what can you do for them?*

16. Use small step ladders

There is a bit of a myth surrounding creating your own destiny and being creative, whether it is for a new business or some other new start for yourself, that somehow you need a 'Big Idea'. The notion is that if you want to be a green shoot you have to have this big inspiration at the heart of your seed.

The myth is compounded in the media with programmes such as BBC TV's *'Dragons Den'* or Sky TV's *'The Big Idea'*.

The standard script goes like this: you have this great idea, so profoundly good, that if only you could get the chance to present it to others, who have a magic wand - or cash for investment - or media exposure – or a celebrity involved, then all will be well.

The truth is somewhat different. The truth is, the 'Big Idea' does not exist.

Sure there have been many ideas and inventions that have subsequently generated great added value, wealth and impact on the world. Yet the creation of any idea, new business product or service, or new life choice is the result of many, many small steps, which in retrospect can add up to a 'Big Idea'.

Potentially great ideas are often billed as, 'The greatest thing since sliced bread'. Yet, even when sliced bred was introduced to the market it was a commercial flop.

In 1912 Otto Frederick Rohwedder invented the first automatic bread slicing machine. Instead of being seen as the greatest thing since sliced gruel the invention was initially a flop, because bakers, felt sliced bread would quickly go stale. Not until 1928, when Rohwedder finally designed a slicer that would also wrap the bread, did he meet with commercial success.

To be successful you do need to think big. Your bigness is characterised by, having a 'Big Vision', or as I prefer to call it a 'Big Bungee Vision'. Your vision is a sense of horizon of where you want to be going, and where your destination lies.

Creativity fundamentally works in the same way as if you were making a snowball. It is an incremental dynamic where you add one thing to another, and another, and another.... Every idea you create is a stepping stone to take you somewhere different.

Nature works in very much the same way. Many, many minute changes at every step of development create the profound diversity of the world around us. Remember the paper-tearing exercise described in Chapter 2, where the slightest variation can lead to significant differences?

Humans share 96 per cent of the DNA of chimpanzees. Welcome to the power of small steps. It's precisely why you are different from a chimpanzee . It's also the way to be flexibly faster.

In my talks on creativity I introduce a bit of theatre into the presentation, when I invite two members of the audience to take part in an exercise. I usually make sure one of the 'volunteers' is the most macho in the group. I give an instruction to the macho delegate to put their feet together and see how far they can leap in one stride.

I act as if to repeat the instruction, but at the very last

second make one significant change; instead of making one leap with feet together, I ask the second volunteer to make the journey by putting one foot in front of the other and keep going.

Who gets the furthest, the one big leap or the many small steps?

It's a bit of silly theatre during a talk but vividly demonstrates the fundamental – you get further with many small steps than one big massive action.

If you want to be a seed of a grass shoot, it doesn't require you to have a Big Idea. What it does need is for you to be flexible, responsive and adaptive to the world around you by making many small changes.

Making small steps is far less frightening than making big ones. It's far easier, and also gives you more options, for example to shuffle to the right or left, forwards or backwards rather than to make just one massive leap forward.

An ugly, unhelpful question to ask yourself, if you want to be a green shoot, is: 'What Big Idea can I use?' This immediately puts any prospective idea on a pedestal. It makes you less tolerant of Ideapoo - those pearls of ideas hidden within an ugly oyster shell.

To adapt the Gershwin brothers song:

'They all laughed at Christopher Columbus, when he said the world was round,
They would have said his mind was not sound,
If he said he would discover this place called America

which would grow into the world's most powerful country....'

OK the last bit does not quite scan to George and Ira's standards. But Columbus did not set sail for 'America'. His mission was to find another route to China. (Also a bit of a truthiness myth, perpetuated by the Gershwin brothers, is that Columbus debunked the myth of a flat earth. With extraordinarily few exceptions, no educated person in the history of Western Civilization from the third century B.C. onward believed that the earth was flat, with most bought into the prevailing view being of a spherical earth.)

Great discoveries are more often the result of stumbling around rather than landing on the precise spot conceived in an idea.

Should you be tougher on yourself than Columbus was on himself, when considering what journey you are going to make to become a green shoot. Are you waiting for Satnav guidance to take you to a specific destination, or are you just going to set sail, and set a course towards what you believe to be the right thing to do?

Demanding an instant, immediate Big Idea hampers, or can even prevent the potential idea from growing. It creates anxiety and unhelpful stress, further restricting your ability to spot opportunities and respond effectively.

Sure, people can have moments of insight, a flash of inspiration. I call these illuminations. And yet even these can have an incremental journey. You will never have a flash of inspiration about a subject you know nothing about. You will always have some core information about your problem, followed by a period of what is called incubation.

Nature also works by following lines of least resistance; a river does not flow in a straight line. In your strategy you don't need to identify the straightest line between you and your objective. You need to identify lines of least resistance.

These lines of least resistance are identified by the easiest small step forward. By being prepared to make many different probes forward – and also being flexible enough to go back and start another route if necessary, you can overcome the biggest obstacles.

How do you eat an elephant? One bite at a time is the old gag, but it's perfectly true in your gameplan when tackling any big task you face.

One of the key reasons why an idea, a new business venture, or a lifestyle change is unsuccessful is that you may have been required to make too many unbridgeable steps. Equally, it may have required the prospective user, customer or person to say an immediate 'Yes' to your idea, to travel too far for their small steps.

When you have an idea in your head, the tendency is for it to be in concrete detail in your mind. The picture is a vivid, yet self-contained vision. But it fails to take into account the niggling little things, the minor interventions, hurdles and diversions that people have to overcome to also get to your destination.

Whenever you have an idea you need to ask yourself a beautiful question: 'What are the small steps I need to ask people to make?'

You can diagnose the optimum step ladder for people to reach the place where you are at.

To get people to take action I believe you need to address five beautiful questions, what I call the '5 star action questions':

1. *How do you make it important? What is it you need to do to increase its significance and make it truly important?*

    Even if you succeed in making people realize that whatever you are asking them to do is important, they still won't act until you address the further four questions.

2. *How do you make it urgent?*

    You need to structure your task so that action is needed now. No matter how important your product or service will be to its user, unless there is an element of urgency – 'order now before this happens' - they will either not press the button to go ahead, or will defer and avoid the decision or expense.

    Even then, they still may not act until you ask the following three questions.

3. *How do you make what you are asking people to do appear low risk?*

People do not buy the best. They buy the least risk. The number of times I have lost new business pitches because I failed to remember this fundamental dictum!

In what ways can you reduce the anxiety people may experience in their decision-making? People don't stop buying in a downturn – they just buy more safely.

Apparently, gentlemen's shirt maker Charles Tyrwhitt is selling more white shirts during the recession, and they put this down to the need to conform. A beautiful question to ask yourself whenever you are selling your idea for a green shoot is: 'How do I make this 'white shirt proof'? (i.e. make it seem safe.)

4. *How do you offer small steps between where your prospect is now, and where you want he, or she to go?* You need to offer small steps to get them to be where you want them to be. What nudges, default options or different ways you can hand things on a plate, to make it unavoidable that they will start down the path of getting to 'Yes' to your want?

5. *How do you offer a quick win?* How can you demonstrate an instant or speedy return on their decision to say 'Yes'?

The same process can also be adapted if you have to defend your status quo, to stop or deter people from moving away from your service, using what I call the '5 star inertia questions'.

1. *How can you relate what you offer to a non-negotiable value the person holds?* Is it for example, quality service - their wanting to be the best employer around? From experience I find the most common mistake is to think that because you see your product or service as important you assume other people automatically feels the same. Don't assume.

2. *How can you make it less urgent for them to move away from you and your product?* Can you identify other priorities they may face - which you can make more evident - which should take precedence over you?

3. *How do you highlight the big risks which will result as a consequence of their not using you?*

4. *What big steps do they need to take? How do you make it costly, time consuming and over complicated to disengage with you?*

5. *What quick losses would be evident as a result of not using you?*

When you are selling your idea for a green shoot, small steps can be used to create extra detail about what you are offering.

What sounds more tempting?

'A cup of coffee.'

or...

At your local Coffeebucks, we serve an incredible variety of handcrafted coffee and espresso beverages. Some use time-honoured recipes. Some are new creations straight from our kitchens. All are delicious. Don't forget to customise your beverage to just the way you like it. Select your size and which milk you would like. Add an extra shot or a delicious syrup, or for a real treat, why not add whipped cream?'

When looking at the detail of your situation, explore beyond its immediate features, identify its benefits – what it does for you, both on a practical and emotional level and the inter-relationship between different elements of your situation.

In what ways can you go the extra yard compared to what is already being offered?

What niches are there to the left or the right, foreground or rear of your situation can you take advantage of?

As this is the first recession with the internet, it provides you with the opportunity to easily to get new information and make connections, and even identify job opportunities. Just a small click away, is a world waiting to be used by you.

Having an attitude of abundance and repeatedly doing many small things for people creates opportunities. Research shows it usually requires seven quality contacts before people will pay for your new service.

Being doing lots of small things you can afford to be generous. By being generous you are actually creating luck for other people.

Luck flows back to sources of luck. I remember on my first day at university, where I spent my entire term's grant. Most of it was admittedly sensible stuff, like hall of residence fees. But the £5 left I spent at the student bar and bought some new-found friends a drink. On the last day of term, skint, I got approached by two people who said: *"I owe you a drink from the first day of term!"*

I am a great fan of using networking, viral, social media, and word of mouth for spreading messages and creating change in the world. The idea of six degrees of separation – how we are just six handshakes away from anyone on this planet – was inspired by a study in 1967 by Stanley Milgram.

He asked 160 people in Nebraska to get a letter to a stockbroker in Boston, passing it only to someone they knew on first-name terms.

The popular story records how the letters arrive after six steps. Yet, the reality was that 80 per cent of the parcels did not arrive.

Follow-up experiments seem to verify this experience; a recent BBC documentary recreating Milgram's experiment saw an even a greater attrition rate on successful deliveries, with only three out of its 40 parcels arriving.

Before you start throwing the baby out with the bathwater here, Milgram's concept of six degrees of separation is still very valid.

The lesson here is not to disprove the theory of six degrees of separation, but the reality of the mechanics in the process; yes you are six degrees away from anyone, but for your message to succeed - to tangibly establish the fact - you need a bulk of the traffic lights to be on Green.

The lessons for viral communications is in order to be effective you cannot put all your eggs into one basket, so to speak. You need a multitude of activity, simultaneously trying several different routes, probably with an attrition rate of anything between 80-95 per cent, before it is successful. Also remember to give other people a reason to pass on your message; you could use flattery or even a freebie of some sort.

When being asked about response rates for direct marketing activity, and what sort of percentage rate you should expect, I always reply: *"It depends on the proposition, the quality of your database, and how you deliver the message; if I was offering a group of known contacts a gift of £50,000 from a newly acquired lottery win, communicated in a nicely written handwritten letter, I would expect to get a 100 per cent response."* (Pity the poor person whose letter gets lost in the post!)

"If however, I as a bank offering a new credit card, with no special offers, where there was no relationship or brand awareness, I am likely to get a response of significantly less than .01 per cent."

The powerful lesson again is of small step thinking.

By taking many small steps, and initially exploring as many different opportunities, channels and contacts as possible, you can overcome the inherent inefficiencies of the viral medium.

The theory of six degrees of separation still hold good.
Pass it on - but don't just rely on one person to pass your
message on – and make many small steps.

Making, consuming and experiencing as many small
steps as possible expands the range of opportunities
available to you and gives you more to think flexibly
around.

Taking small steps helps your flexible thinking move
quicker. It can also bring you dividends for your green
shoot when you least expect.

Your green shoot Action Steps

1.   *What small steps do people need to take before saying 'Yes' to you?*

2.   *When someone says 'No' to you, is there still some aspect of what you offer which would be of interest to them?*

3.   *What is the line of least resistance in making your green shoot happen? What is the very least you could or should do?*

4.   *How can you make your green shoot idea 'whiteshirt proof'? Use the 5 Star Action step questions to make your idea happen. Are you selling coffee, or a story?*

5.   *How can you give to, and harness the potential of your immediate networks, to enable them to help you reach out to the wider world with your green shoot idea?*

17. Elasticate your life

To think flexibly faster you need to elasticate your life.

Rather like a rubber band that adapts, stretches and consolidates when necessary, your daily actions need to have a similar responsiveness.

You need a regular diet of flexibility in your life to boost your responsiveness.

The more you treat flexible responses as the norm, the more ready and alert you will be. It's a bit like taking your responsiveness to the gym and making it more supple, agile and strong.

Doing lots of new things is exercise for your brain. The neurons in your brain are wired to respond to novel events, and not to fire if events do not provide new information. Being flexible in your daily habits gives your neurons a fresh work out.

Each of us has a comfort zone, which demarcates between the things in life we find comfortable doing, and other tasks which can fill us with unease at the very thought of them. The bigger your comfort zone, the more likely it will embrace different challenges and new things that life will throw at you.

You also have a complacency zone, marking out territory in your life where you, frankly, don't give a damn, or at least cannot be bothered to do anything. This area of indifference, marks the areas you fail to, or are disinclined to act.

For many, the regular job and paycheque has created a complacency zone, creating a comfort of not taking responsibility for your future, or acting as a golden handcuff to stop you creating a better future for you.

Some people I have met are old before their time. They may not have grey hair or wrinkles, but their 'age' is marked by being set in their ways.

Age should not be measured in years, but more by a responsiveness to new things, new challenges and new opportunities.

For many, their comfort zone shrinks as they get older. They will only do things if they are absolutely exactly as they want them. A friend of mine had to complete a 500 mile round trip to pick up their elderly parent, who was only prepared to travel in daylight, so they could see out of the window during the journey!

I once flew first class on a business trip to Dubai. The sheer luxury and non-stop pampering was most enjoyable. Less satisfying was listening to the non-stop whingeing of the passenger next to me.

Although she still got on the plane in good time, the special chauffeur home pick-up service was delayed. The tardy chauffeur, her drink not quite right, and her recliner chair not having the right angle of incline all became the focus of her conversation for the whole flight.

I reckoned she had a far less enjoyable flight than someone cooped in whatever the worst conditions of economy class could throw at them. Despite consuming a service costing considerably more than the lowest price ticket she was resolutely unhappy (she hadn't even paid for the flight herself and apparently, 'always flew first class'.)

One reason for her not fully realizing, or savouring her moment of luxury was that First Class had become her norm, her standard default, within which there should be no variation.

She was suffering from Parkinson's Second Law where expenditure rises to meet income, coupled with a bad bout of 'Affluenza'. The need for the first class ticket was not driven by an appreciation of the comfort, but by the habit of living a life to the maximum materialistic cost.

Had she lived a more flexible life, maybe on occasions flying economy, she would have been far more appreciative of the real experience, and certainly been more robust when things hadn't gone to plan.

By adopting flexibility in your consumer habits whether it experiencing is an airline flight both first class and economy, staying in both youth hostels and luxury hotels, eating out at roadside cafes or having gourmet diners, or shopping at charity shops and designer boutiques (you can sometimes combine the two) you will be constantly expanding your comfort zone. You will be making it more elastic. And you will enjoy more what you consume.

Having no fear of discomfort gives you a luxury, an advantage over others who live life in a pampered single dimension.

The downside of being on a Hedonistic treadmill is that causes you to rapidly and inevitably adapt to good things by taking them for granted. As you accumulate more wealth and material possessions, your expectations rise.

Apparently, self made millionaires are four times more likely to be dyslexic. My theory is that by living a life in which even simple words may be interpreted in different ways, makes the dyslexic mind more agile and flexible and able to spot and respond to opportunities.

Your flexible daily living should also incorporate going beyond being you in the moment: you can draw inspiration from your ancestors surviving the Black Death, from your self when you successfully dealt with an earlier adverse situation, or from using inspiring role models.

Being alive is an extraordinary piece of good luck and achievement on your part. Don't forget to celebrate yourself at appropriate times each day.

Your daily flexibility should span being both pessimistic and optimistic when evaluating your reality. Even bad days need to be recognised as good days in disguise – where you can learn something new every day.

Try using a foreign language to briefly describe something you have done or are about to do. Challenge yourself to translate as quickly as possible, as if you were talking to someone and wanted to appear a fluent speaker. Speeding up thinking tasks like this can help you to think faster in other areas of your life.

Your daily flexibility should include a flexible cultural experience. When was the last time you visited a museum or art gallery, (or other than this one), read a book?

And a flexible 'cultural experience' can be something as simple as dipping into a different radio station, newspaper, TV channel, or web site.

You should do something fashionable – and unfashionable. (The latter I'm particularly good at.) Indeed, introducing some nostalgia in your life – although it will never as be a good as it used to be – can be good for your health.

A study by psychologist Ellen Langer in 1979 took a group of elderly men on a virtual time travel journey. They had to listen, live and talk as if they were living twenty years earlier, in 1959.

Compared to the control group the men's health was significantly improved. By turning the time travel clock back, they had also adjusted their psychological clock. Maybe, you could do some time travelling in your daily schedule.

What about wearing your watch, or jewellery on a different hand?

Write something using your other hand.

Your daily flexibility should include a random act of kindness. The comedy writer and TV host Danny Wallace wrote a book called *'Yes Man'*, where he had to spend six months saying 'Yes' to everything.

I used to run a gallery at a media centre in Wakefield. Unaware of his latest quest I inadvertently e mailed him to ask if we could do an exhibition on his current book *'Join Me!'* - on how he set up a one man cult based on doing random acts of kindness. And guess what his response to my e mail was?

In launching the exhibition, Danny not only said 'Yes' but decided to go around Wakefield city centre doing random acts of kindness for strangers. The effects were amazing; the demeanours of the dourest of passers-by were transformed by a simple, unprompted gift of a sweet.

The life of both the giver and receiver were momentarily changed – providing a different dimension to each of their days.

I do like creative artist Keri Smith's shopping list of things you can do every day to help your efforts to be an explorer:

- start a collection or start a new collection
- change routes or routines – have breakfast first before showering.
- observe for long and short spells
- notice patterns
- create connections – trace things back to their origins
- make notes
- observe the world as if you haven't seen it before
- recognize there is no correct way of understanding anything
- look for new things in junk mail, overheard conversations, colours, knots
- think about and enjoy your childhood memories
- create an alphabet every day of 26 new things you notice beginning with each letter of the alphabet

Variety can be fun. Equally you may need to add the opposite in your life to equip you with the challenges you face.

In a follow-up discussion at one of my talks, a delegate observed how current education practices, where lessons are delivered, so to speak on a plate, are in danger of creating a generation of attention-seeking, needy, over-confident, comfortable people who are not prepared for certain realities of life, including how work can be tedious, boring and mundane. To prepare and equip them for a working life ahead, he felt these realities need to be addressed in some way. (I made the suggestion that such classes could be called 'Tedia Studies'.)

Try the menu of Daily Surprises in the Appendix to this book to give your flexibility the equivalent of a gym work-out to expand your Flexibility Quotient.

Flexibility primes your mind to look out for more, both to spot the initial opportunity, then to engage with it and try it out in some way. In our thinking we have what medical researchers call an Index of Reference which provides you with the parameters of your vision; the wider it is the more you see.

Yet, sadly, many people wouldn't know a stroke of luck if it bit them on the nose.

Some people who may be labelled 'creative' may not like conventional rules, but can still be rigidly hide bound in non-conventional areas of their lives. I have a theory that the more outrageously you express yourself in one dimension of your life, the more you counter balance this with extreme conservatism in mode of thinking in other areas.

In my work as a creativity consultant, the most inflexible thinkers I have found were either groups of artists, or people involved in hazardous sports; put them in their artistic medium or in extreme conditions and they will brilliantly respond, adapt and adjust to new challenges.

Outside of these situations however, in spite of outstanding divergence in one aspect of their lives, they seem to counter-compensate for this with an extreme reluctance and conservatism and reluctance to be flexible in other areas of their life. They have become dogmatic beyond their niche.

Orson Welles' quote from the film *'The Third Man'*, is a great example of flexible creative thinking by making small steps and being flexible.

During the filming they realised extra dialogue was needed in a scene to fill out the space. Orson Welles was a very well educated man. Drawing upon his vast library of reading he came up with a solution.

Welles claimed a book written by the artist Whistler inspired these lines. The original version was:

> *'The Swiss in their mountains ... What more worthy people! ... yet, the perverse and scornful [Goddess, Art] will none of it, and the sons of patriots are left with the clock that turns the mill, and the sudden cuckoo, with difficulty restrained in its box! For this was Tell a hero! For this did Gessler die!'*

He flexibly responded to the new situation, and created a brilliant solution.

I have yet to meet anyone who can remember any other quotes from the film.

Welles was also flexible with the facts: he later recalled in his autobiography how: *"When the picture came out, the Swiss very nicely pointed out to me that they've never made any cuckoo clocks."* Even a great philomath like Welles didn't eschew the tabloid adage of not letting the facts get in the way of a good story.

In the age of the Internet, you don't necessarily need to have Welles' encyclopaedic knowledge to find similar solutions. We can outsource parts of our brain to Google. A few clicks on the Internet and you have access to a library far vaster than Orson could lay his hands on.

This is the first recession with the Internet, so you can make use of its vast potential, and the flexible use of its resources will help transform your journey considerably.

Even if you feel you are living a rather plain or living a humdrum life, by having a strong sense of who you are, where you want to be - coupled with doing lots of small steps and enjoying daily doses of flexibility in your life −your prospects of becoming a green shoot be enhanced considerably.

The person who has more options has more power – and more power to create and sustain their green shoot.

There still are however, other challenges to face, if you want to think flexibly faster.

Your green shoot Action Steps

1. *To make you more flexible in facing the green shoot opportunities which will come your way do something different today to stretch your Comfort and Complacency Zones. (At the very least, look at your world from a different angle in some way.)*

2. *In what ways can you incorporate both living first class (this may not actually cost money) and ultra-budget?*

3. *Identify something that makes you feel uncomfortable. Create discomfort by doing something involving your personal hell.*

4. *Go and do something you have not done before; visit an art gallery, a museum, do a sport or visit a shop you would not normally go to, or read a book, magazine or watch a TV show you would not normally entertain in order to stimulate new ideas.*

5. *Say 'Yes' to more things today (including doing a random act of kindness) to help you on your way to becoming a green shoot.*

18. Flush out the crap

Being a prospective green shoot in the recovery is time consuming.

Your speed of response to new opportunities and challenges is going to be hampered by the age old complaint – 'I don't have enough time!'

I suspect you, like every single person I have ever met, are time poor - and you are finding that it is getting worse.

I have yet to meet anyone who has lots of spare time – especially when they are asked to do something.

We live in an age of desperate poverty – the poverty of time. (Apart from the 'Twixtmas' period - between the Christmas and the New Year holidays - where people often complain of not knowing what to do.)

In your quest to become a green shoot, you need time and space around you.

To achieve this you need to do four things:

- Get rid of unnecessary stuff, clutter, in your life
- Do what you have to, but do it quicker or in less time
- Be a dating agency between the hours and minutes required for a task and your available time.
- Focus on the key quality which will make your green shoot outstanding

Firstly, you need to get rid of things. Stuff that actually does not do anything for you.

As a trainer I have never come across a venue which did not boast its collection of used felt pens. I always check the pens work before starting a course. Invariably, many of the pens have run out of ink. Why keep them? They are useless and just clutter up your world. It would be good if they could be recycled. But just lying dormant, waiting to irritate the next person who picks them up is not doing anyone any good.

What is the equivalent of the used felt pen in your life?

Earlier in my career I worked at the Yorkshire Water Authority, then a publicly owned utility. I was told about how the Authority used to employ a team of motorcyclists whose job every morning was to visit the remotest of reservoirs, in some of the most beautiful parts of Yorkshire, to quickly check the reservoir dam, just to make sure it had not suddenly fallen down.

The job certainly achieved its objective; the Authority was able to check each day if its dams had not overnight revealed a massive crack or crumbled away.

During the water industry strike of 1976 the Authority's managers were faced with trying to maintain public water supplies with the barest of resources. They faced the real life equivalent of a creativity game I use for managers: *"If you had to run your business from a phone box what would you do?"*

Faced with a need to do only the absolutely urgent and essential, the job of going up to the reservoirs each day got dropped.

Once the strike was settled it was realized that some jobs may not have been necessary after all. Sure, the dams do need regular safety inspections. Yet, a visit every day?

If a problem is going to occur it will be a major structural one, evident over a long period of time. If an immediate catastrophe occurs or something crashes into a dam, would people need to wait for the motorcycle spotter to do their daily visit and spread the alert?

What is the equivalent of the daily inspection of the dam in your life? What can you do without, or less frequently? What does not matter a damn if it gets done or not?

If you do not address this equivalent of a regular spring clean in your life – not just of your home and wardrobe – but of your daily schedule - it will continue to create clutter and hold you back. It will be like trying to lead a cavalry charge when you still have to drag a cart behind you with all your possessions.

Parkinson's First Law states that work expands to fill the time available for its completion. People need to operate on at least a twin track strategy by adopting what I call 'the Black Sock strategy', so named after I discovered a thief in my house; every time we did the laundry a sock would go missing.

After spending some time playing at being a sock dating agency, pairing up different socks, I felt this was not good use of my time. I figured my gravestone was not going to laud my ability to wear matching socks.

My answer to preventing further waste of my precious

time was to wear black socks. I'll let you into a secret, often they may not be the same precise pair of black socks. But I get away with it. My rough and ready solution gives me sufficient added value.

Now, if you are exploring new ideas and opportunities for your future green shoot, it will inevitably take up time. But people don't have spare time. So the answer is to adopt the black sock strategy.

The story about my black socks is a bit facile. But it's even more stupid wasting your most precious resource, your time. Your first personal resource management task is to ask this beautiful question: *"What is the equivalent to the black socks in my life? What can I do fastercheaperbetter - and dirtier if need be, without compromising my core quest?"*

You will find there is much that can be automated, repeated, delegated or even abdicated. We can choose to rush and be busy. We can also choose to slow down and cut back. Walk away from stuff not requiring your silver service response and give it instead, the black sock treatment.

We all know that death and taxes are the two certainties of life. And tax is not just in money. But also time. Anytime any public official engages with you they are actually levying a further tax. On your time.

The time it takes to complete an official form is a time tax.

A particular bugbear of mine is public sector tender procedures, where anyone interested in securing significant public contracts has to jump through a series of hoops in order to be considered.

We do of course need proper checks and systems. The reality is that technological changes have become more sophisticated - with the Internet, many more people can be aware of potential opportunities. What has not changed in parallel is the sophistication of managing the process.

Be a time tax collector on yourself and how others impact upon you. You need to cultivate the uncommon habit of making decisions, both for yourself and others. Be ruthless and avoid being a time tax burden on those around you. Eliminate before you delegate.

It is a pity that none of the major political parties will make an issue of, and pledge themselves to cutting back on time tax.

Will the Upturn see an increase of people judged by the results they deliver, not their obedience to be at a certain place for a certain period of time?

Will the cult of effectiveness, of doing the things that get you closer to your goals, be celebrated and better recognised in the workplace? With limited resources you need to focus – and focus specifically on what is the point of difference you are making in the world.

What we fear doing most is usually what we need to do. Do you find you are inventing things to do to avoid the important?

In his book *‘Eat that frog!’* Brian Tracy calls the tasks you keep fobbing off and not doing, as your ‘frog jobs’. The trick is to ‘eat the frog’ and do these first in your planned schedule for the day. Before the downturn it was easier to avoid eating the frogs. You now need a lizard-like rapacity for frogs if you are going to be part of the Upturn.

Shortening your work time by choice, or by being forced to as a result of the downturn, can help you focus on the important, and to work on this, and this alone. It makes you identify what is your personal 80/20 rule (where, as Pareto observed, 80 per cent of your results come from just 20 per cent of your input.)

As a general rule I would suggest reviewing your activities with a target of identifying 80 per cent of your tasks which can be done quicker and dirtier.

Using the time freed up from doing the bulk of things quicker or dirtier you can invest this time dividend into the crucial things, the 20 per cent of things which can make a profound difference to your green shoot prospects.

There is an apocryphal story about a manager who was faced with a massive pile of job applications. Overwhelmed, they realised they would not have sufficient time to adequately sift through and make a considered judgment to discover the best candidate.

Their response was to divide the pile into two and throw half the applications away, leaving a manageable batch to process. Observing this a colleague remonstrated: *"How can you just throw away half of the applications without looking at them?"* To which the decisive manager replied: *"You wouldn't want to employ anyone unlucky would you?"*

A comical story, obviously far fetched. Is it any sillier, however, than the actions of one major government funded initiative which had the task of providing grants for creative people to realise their dreams.

Following up why my application was unsuccessful, I was told: *"You did not include the separate CV as requested in the paperwork."*

I remonstrated as to why the junior administrative person dealing with the initial process couldn't quickly drop me an e mail requesting the additional details.

On reflection, I realised they were just using this as a crude tool to sift down their numbers. The experience led me to provide them with what I thought was constructive feedback: *"If you guys had been in charge of the Sistine Chapel commission, Michelangelo probably wouldn't have got the job!"*

Sure, they needed to manage their numbers. But how many potential pearls did they fail to discover by using irrelevant criteria; their quest was to find future stars, not exceptional pen pushers.

You need to be flexible in your management of tasks. Maybe you need several stages of sifting rather than just one. What quick and dirty measures can you introduce to impose the least time tax on you, and others?

The paradox of modern technology, often referred to as the 'Crackberry syndrome' – where we crave connectivity and speed, is also when we risk turning ourselves into busy fools, bamboozled by too much noise and information.

A wealth of information creates a poverty of attention. It is a bit like having your music player on so loud that you can't really understand or appreciate the lyrics, or even enjoy the song: It becomes noise rather than music.

A recent survey by Cranfield and Northampton business schools revealed that around a quarter of 1,200 professionals spent three or more hours a day on their e mails and sending text messages. More than half the younger and middle aged respondents never switch their phones off.

Being busy is a form of laziness. Because you are not actively managing your time and priorities your lazy thinking leads to indiscriminate action. Ask yourself; are you being productive or just active?

Sure, it is important to be connected, but you need to distinguish between more connected with more distracted. Are we just choosing not to choose?

It is not simply wishing all the extra information away, but learning to deal with what's important and what is 'Noisepoo' - stuff that clutters up and doesn't constructively add to your universe.

Are you a slave to e mail? Do you instantly check and respond? What if you just checked one every hour, day, week?

Break down the elements of what an e mail communication consists of. It can be an urgent alert. Imagine Batman receiving dozens of calls on his Bat phone relating to every bit of police activity in Gotham City.

Could you envisage the Caped Crusader picking up the call and clicking his bat heels while saying to Robin, the Boy Wonder: *"Oh, it's just another neighbourhood watch call Robin, reporting something slightly suspicious. We won't respond."*

No, the one call he gets is just the one he needs to take, so he can make best use of his resource. What is the equivalent of your Bat phone?

Meetings can be an immense time tax burden. Are the meetings essential for the optimum performance of you or your team? Or are they more about power, for someone to show who is in charge by calling them? What about having a new rule in your life of not making any meeting compulsory? Anyone attending will be there because they judge it is best use of their time.

Do you insist that meetings only be held to make a decision about a predefined situation, not to define the problem? If someone asks for a meet, do you ask the person to send an agenda to define the purpose? In the age of the Upturn you need to discipline yourself and others.

Brainstorming meetings can be similarly wasteful. What is the point of getting a group of people together to come up with the obvious, or ideas you would have come up with anyway?

Brainstorms – which by the way, is a politically correct expression - can be an effective creativity tool to stretch the team's thinking, to redefine problems by engaging a group of people rather than using just a single mind.

Far too often however, brainstorm meetings are used as a panic signal to indicate a new threat or challenge. They are often a lazy response from the person who owns the problem; by calling the brainstorm as a first response they abdicate responsibility for taking initial individual action. They would save everyone else time by working on the problem initially by themselves.

You need to manage your incubation, using every opportunity to sleep on problems and let your mind multi task on several different things at once.

'Pre meets', the preliminary meetings to prepare for action can also be a costly burden. Maybe they should be called 'Indecision, or lack of self belief time tax' meetings. Cut them out by forcing people to make decisions, or replace them with a phone call or teleconference.

Give people a mandated choice. If they don't make a decision, you make the decision for them.

Apparently, to increase the rate of body organ donation the driving licence application form simply needs to be tweaked. The Government should only accept and process applications if people have actually answered the organ donation question it features. At present, most people ignore it. (People would still of course have the choice to say 'No'.)

How can you similarly nudge people, with the minimum of effort, to support your green shoot?

In the world of high-street fashion, most actually wear black.

If you are offered 57 flavours of ice-cream most go for chocolate or vanilla.

What defaults can you set in your life and how can you overcome other people's indecisiveness by minimising the number of decisions your customers have to make.

Giving people choice is not about shades of options. The Ford Model T was available in any colour, as long as it was black; the freedom of choice was created by making car ownership available to the mass market. (I once did a creativity training session with Ford, where I discovered the 'any colour in black' story wasn't strictly true. The Model T was actually available in black or green options, but for a period of two weeks they were out of stock of green paint, which prompted Henry Ford's comment.)

In your quest to provide a different service for your seed idea to the potential customer, there is a danger over-elaborating and over-gilding what you do.

Your job is not to wipe people's bottoms, although that could possibly be a market opportunity, particularly in the care sector.

Customer service is about providing an excellent product, at an acceptable price while solving your customers' legitimate needs in the easiest way possible for them. You need a beautiful question: *"What exactly is the bottom line here?"* (no pun intended.)

Another bugbear of mine, which will hopefully be flushed away by the Upturn, is the almost religious adherence some decision-makers have to scoring systems when making a decision.

They are somehow regarded as 'scientific' and 'objective' because they identify a set range of factors and give numerical scores on each dimension. Baloney!

Yes, a scoring system is a good tool for helping you identify key criteria and also for enabling people to articulate their intuitions; but then people simply start fiddling, adjusting the figures and weightings to justify their gut feeling

In group situations, where people are seemingly afraid of making decisions and being accountable, there is a tendency to dutifully abide by whatever numerical value is created in the exercise.

Use scoring systems as tools but do not abdicate your responsibility to take decisions. Did you use such a scoring system for one of the biggest decisions in your life - selecting a partner?

Your best ideas will often come to you unprompted, out of the blue. I call these 'illuminations'. Capture them. In reality we tend to say: *"That's a good idea, I must make a note of that."* And don't. These illuminations are calls from your unconscious mind. They tend to be the stepping stones for really profound, good quality ideas.

Recognise them. Respect them. And record them.

You need to take control by having a flexible range of responses; at one end of the scale is when you completely switch off, detaching yourself from all around you, so you can recharge your batteries and to help you see the wood for the trees. At the other end of the spectrum - when confronted by a new reality and outstanding opportunity - is the ability to immediately respond with great vigour and speed.

In my creative writing classes I find I am spending more time helping people with time management, because the delegates in their daily work reveal how they will constantly let the phone or e mail interrupt them. They fail to recognise that their writing task is not a quick, instant job, but possibly requires at least 20 minutes of undivided attention free from interruption. People are seemingly working in just one gear when responding to their environment. It is as if they have homogenous thinking, consisting of an instant fast reaction rather than categorizing their energy, focus and time so that they can provide the optimum response and use of their resource.

You need a variety of time slots in your schedule which gives you time to create a masterpiece as well as a Twitter message.

At least one positive of the downturn will be that it forces people and organizations to take intelligent short cuts in their routine activities.

We are witnessing a culture shift away from the regime of employing people to turn up for work between nine and five - and using that as the key measure of their contribution.

Replacing this culture will be what I call the 'Rumpelstiltskin Challenge' – your task is to spin your gold, in whatever way you see fit. Your employer, or customer gives you the target. And you deliver.
You are not employed to watch a clock.

By flushing out things you do not really need to do, doing tasks quicker, cheaper, or dirtier, or focussing on the real premium difference you offer will secure a precious resource, so you can focus on what you really need to be doing to get your green shoot going.

What is the metaphorical toilet chain you can picture yourself flushing to rid your life of some unnecessary clutter?

What is the clutter in your life? What is it that you are 100 per cent accountable for? What are the things where you do not have 100 per cent control over where you are beating yourself up over.

If you did not, or could not have it, what then? What are you going to do to get rid, dump it, delegate it, streamline it, or ignore it?

What is the equivalent of the 'black socks' in your life?

Posing these beautiful questions will give you more time and space to respond flexibly faster.

Having cleared your decks, so to speak, you now need to uncover the key essential difference - the silver service aspect or distinctive dimension of your service or product - which will make your green shoot outstanding.

What do you need to do to focus on this and make the most of your potential?

There is one more crucial thing you need to consider in your quest to think flexibly faster, and become an outstanding green shoot.

Your green shoot Action Steps

1. *What is the clutter (to use a polite word) in your life? How can you get rid, streamline, delegate, or ignore?*

2. *What are the 80 per cent of tasks you can do quicker, dirtier, or not at all?*

3. *How can you pay less Time Tax, and impose less of a Time Tax burden on others?*

4. *What is the equivalent of the Bat phone in your life, alerting you to the real important things?*

5. *How can you apply 'less is more' to your life? What do you really need to focus on in order to become a successful green shoot?*

19. Take massive action

Imagine you were at a casino, and somehow you knew what the next winning number was going to be on the roulette wheel.

Would you just bet your loose change, or would you scrape everything you could lay your hands on to make the most of this sure-fire bet opportunity?

The answer might seem straightforward, yet in real life, when you are faced with a potential winning number, how often do you play it? Do you take massive action to fully exploit it?

All of us are capable of taking massive action. It usually requires an external deadline, a boss or angry customer insistent that you give it all you have got. The quality of outstanding opportunists and superlative green shoots is the ability to take massive action without someone else's deadline looming over them. The deadline is their own.

The *'Daily Telegraph'* ran an advertisement in the summer of 2009 featuring photographs of three unremarkable buildings, consisting of two sheds and a garage.

The remarkable factor was the caption beneath them, indicating they were the home and first workplaces of Harley Davidson, Ikea and Google. Underneath was a headline which read: *'It Pays to Think Big'*.

There seems to be an implication that the size of the thinking was crucial to the subsequent success.

Yet, the ad and its imagery missed the main point. Sure, the three budding companies were, seemingly, examples of having a powerful vision. You too, by having what I call a Big Box view of your destiny can create a powerful tool in your armoury for future success.

Yet, in my work I have met many hundreds of 'failures' with Big Thinking; each had great plans, impressive organizational flow charts, sexy brand logos for their future empire, and even great, sexy buildings as homes for these forward minded Big Thinking businesses.

But none developed into world-beating legends. I am not knocking them for trying. Nor for having their dreams.

The most compelling message of the three images of the sheds and garage however, is something else. The essential ingredients for ensuring future success is based around posing three beautiful questions:

How can you be clearly focussed on your Big Goal, driven by your point of difference, your competitive difference?

How do you harness your resources to this difference, how do you make it the spine of your future success?

How can you now take massive action using whatever resources you have to achieve your goals?

As a result, you scrimp on the non-essentials, such as sexy buildings – like the examples of Harley Davidson, Ikea and Google.

The danger of Big Thinking is the need to balance being focussed on the Big Goal while being mindful of fundamental business realities, such as is the rent on a sexy building affordable or sustainable – and is it an immediate priority anyway?

The phrase *'Big Thinking'* is a memorable, what I call a 'sticky' phrase. It is can easily be used to inspire others.

The alternative headline for the Daily Telegraph adverts could have been: *'Big, clearly focussed thinking on your specific point of difference – and making sure you scrimp on any non-essentials so you can take massive action'* .

It is less word of mouth friendly. It is probably less inspirational, and yet is profoundly more insightful.(I suppose the headline could have been summarised as *'Take Massive Focussed Action'*.)

The financier George Soros is a great example of someone recognising the need and power of massive focussed action. He successfully bet in the world currency markets against the British pound in 1992. Soros assumed, correctly, that the Bank of England would not support the pound indefinitely in the European Exchange Rate Mechanism (ERM) as it would have to increase interest rates in an economy already in recession.

Overnight, Soros made $1 billion when the Bank of England let the British currency devalue. Rather than diversify across hundreds of stocks he took a concentrated position, one ideally with limited downside, but with a huge potential upside.

Taking massive action is not just about moving to the new

future. It can also be about moving away from the past.

Sean Malone runs Yellowspanner a successful family-run events management company in the UK. Sean started the business from scratch, after he decided he wanted to make a new start, despite working for some of the world's biggest blue chip names.

Preparing marketing materials for the new venture, Sean was tempted to use some of his earlier examples of work and testimonials from satisfied clients. It would instantly give the new business a credibility and a pedigree which could take years to accrue. Using this material would be a short-cut.

Sean's daughter however, dug her heels in. If we are making a new start, we are making a new start she told her father. A determined young lady, she even prepared a bonfire to both get rid of the materials and, perhaps with some precocious wisdom, make a statement.

Sean reluctantly put all the old case work of previous clients' work on the bonfire.

Looking back, Sean reflects it was the best thing they could have done. He recognised how it forced him start from new. Any success would be down to the new team, not to former glories. It gave their mission in starting anew a degree of integrity and meaning which, in turn, further fuelled their drive to succeed.

Ancient Greek generals were also known to use the same tactic, burning their boats after they had landed for an invasion. The message for their armies was clear: you succeed or die. Victory is the only option.

It seems many people would rather cling to a burning boat - whether it is a job they are dissatisfied with or a failing business - than vigorously pursue a new dream with vigour.

Sadly, most of us don't have the ready equivalent of a determined daughter to make us do the right thing. Do you need to start making a bonfire for yourself?

What are you holding on to from your past? What can you put on your bonfire?

Unlike George Soros, I have been guilty of failing to take massive action. Two examples to share are my campaign to save the Millennium Bridge wobble and my *'A minute with Tony Blair'* book, both described in Chapter 14.

I still feel I was right to campaign and generate publicity around my belief that the wobble in the Millennium footbridge should be seen as an opportunity, not a problem. To make my case I wrote to several key decision-makers and prominent politicians involved in the decision. Several weeks after the bridge was closed down I issued a news release which generated some coverage about my bid to 'save the wobble'.

On further reflection however, I was guilty of not taking massive action.

The discovery of the wobble and the following decision to close the bridge was a major international story. In hindsight, I should have acted faster and made more of an effort to get my case noticed and seize upon its topicality.

Perhaps, I should have done a set of photocalls on the bridge to draw attention to my cause. I could have even created a *'WobbleFest'* on the bridge - anything to dramatize, engage, and make better known. An on-line petition could have helped others to get behind my crusade. There was much else I could have done to transform a nice example of spotting opportunities into a much better known icon.

My *'A Minute with Tony Blair'* book was a good, well-received idea. It was so well received I should have made it an annual event. Producing new versions of the book each year could have made it a mini-institution, a vibrant icon for collecting famous and ordinary people's political, philosophical or flippant views.

I suspect before reading this book you had not heard of my effort to save the wobble or the *'A Minute with Tony Blair'* book. That might have been different had I taken massive action.

The lessons for responding with massive action, is that you need to act speedily, with as much resource as you can muster. George Soros would not have achieved his financial coup had he decided to dither and just put a small stake down, or had he not got round to doing it until the following day.

You need to be rooted to the spot of your opportunity and ferociously exploit your unique opportunity. It is like being a prospector, finding a nugget and then deciding to potter around on nearby ground rather than digging down to your potential goldmine.

Less is more.

I tried to help someone recently, alerting them to a job offer which sounded fantastic, the ideal job for them. Later, I asked if they had acted on the tip off. They replied that they had sent a CV in. Ultimately, they did not get the job.

In my view, they should have responded with massive action to such a distinct opportunity; getting to know the target company better, doing something to make their CV stand out from the crowd, making contact with any connections for added insight/recommendations/ endorsements, doing whatever it takes to make the best of a less-than-common opportunity.

OK, so you cannot do this with every job application, but it could well be worth while formulating a gameplan of either doing fewer applications or a small step strategy of using a low cost, quicker/dirtier scattergun approach to job opportunities, coupled with a higher grade, premium approach to the special openings you want to make the most of.

Again, flexibility, not one size fits all, is the guiding principle.

My two personal examples of under-exploited opportunities are what I call Base Camp 2 of the creative journey.

At the Base Camp 1 stage you do not have an immediate, ready opportunity. You are looking around for new ideas and potential seams of gold. By having a belief in your mission, being flexible, adaptable, repeatedly probing around your environment, taking many small steps, you create new chances for yourself.

This is your divergent thinking at work.

When however, you come across your potential Golden Swan you need to unleash your convergent thinking, where you stop exploring, and rather like the lucky gold digger, exploit the spot you are in.

Avoid waiting for things to be perfect before acting. To mix our bird metaphors here, you do not need every duck to be in a row before you take action. You just need to make sure you have the essential ducks, the vital ones, critical to your mission, to secure your point of difference and future success.

Your ideas only have value when you act upon them.

Your potential Golden Swan, your great green shoot opportunity, will not be realised unless you move fast and use the equivalent of a sledgehammer, to take massive action.

Carpe Disruption!

Your green shoot Action Steps

1. *How can you go the extra yard with your green shoot opportunity?*

2. *Where do you need to focus your energy and resources to seize your green shoot or Golden Swan opportunity?*

3. *What is your equivalent of Sean Malone's bonfire - where you need to take massive action to clear the decks?*

4. *For what opportunities in the past have you been guilty of failing to take massive action? What lessons would you take from the experience to apply to your challenge of becoming a green shoot?*

5. *Where is your potential goldmine? Where do you need to start digging?*

Section IV – coming to the end of my part

This book is in two parts.

The first part in which you have just read is a primer to prepare you for the second part.

The second part however, remains to be written.

It is your book, your story, and your tale of how you are going to create your own green shoot to play a part in the Upturn. You need to write it.

Like a seed in nature, the specific trigger for someone to either take action in response to events around them, or to start realizing their inner dreams - and so become a green shoot in the economic recovery, is still a mystery.

Although at the time of writing, fears of a financial meltdown witnessed during 2008 and early in 2009 appear to have abated, it is likely we will still have a general slowdown of the economy for some time.

While there is valid criticism of mistakes made by Governments in the run up to the credit crisis and the resultant downturn, they appear to have demonstrated the key qualities of speed and responsiveness; whether they have done the right thing still remains to be seen.

The greatest rewards in this age of disruption will go those who move fast. In the age of disruption the tough don't just have to get going, they need to get going faster. This new age will be unkind to the slow of thought and rigid of mind. You too, need to show the qualities of speed and responsiveness.

Hubris, a sense of blind and deaf arrogance, particularly among the financial community, got us into this mess of global economic meltdown. There was a false faith in seemingly new ways of financial management, where risk could be calculated and managed to the *nth* degree. Where even toxic assets could be sold on, and on. Mixed with a dose of 'truthiness' - with financial experts believing what they wanted to believe - a great economic calamity was created.

Hibris, a sense of positive belief in your own abilities, coupled with humility, a willingness to be flexible and to learn from even the unlikeliest of sources is your best response to the world economic crisis.

The mission of this book was compared in the introduction with the Oscar winning film *'Slumdog Millionaire'* in its task to be a feelgood book - albeit one grounded in the real realities of recession-hit Britain.

I had the pleasure of meeting the film's director Danny Boyle. When asked what you can do to get a break in the film industry his response was valid for any career: *"If success was a big door with a big illuminated sign saying, 'Success here' you would bet there would be a long queue. You would also be sure that the rich would be at the front of it."*

Because there is no door with an illuminated sign, life does somehow tend to reward skill, effort and resourcefulness. If you can invest in your human bandwidth, your ability to take more on and be able to respond quicker, and be determined to make the most of your abilities then it will serve you well in your quest to be a green shoot in the Upturn.

You have already been resourceful in reading this book.

By using different tools for guidance you will be able to think more flexibly by:

- having a pit stop to stock up on your pessimism and understand and be prepared for any worst case scenarios

- launching into the unknown with your equivalent of a bungee rope, to take you to your scary vision – and bring you back again

- being proud of a medal from your collection, using it to give you strength when you need it and to bounce back when someone says 'No'

- using beautiful boxes to house your beautiful questions and address the real issues in any situation, to give you better insight than those making the same assumptions as everyone else

- checking your Martini clock – to remind you that opportunities are any time, any place, anywhere

Yet in the age of disruption you not only need to think flexibly, you need to think flexibly faster by using the tools of:

- being a living magnet to attract opportunities to you

- using a small step ladder to create as many connections with different things and places around you

- introducing more elasticity in your daily schedule so you can flexibly respond quicker and more flexibly

- ruthlessly pulling at the metaphorical toilet chain in your life, flushing the unnecessary away, and also using a 'black sock strategy' to simplify, do quicker, smarter, or easier for the other, less important things

- having the equivalent of a sledgehammer to take massive action when the right Golden Swan moment comes along

What are you going to do differently? What is going to be the trigger for you to take action?

Even in nature there are seeds that have the right soil, water and temperature but still refuse to grow. There will be many people out there who will remain passive victims of the global downturn, and refuse to grow.

Your trigger for change might be a desire to prove someone wrong, peer-pressure, wanting to make money, or wanting to be perceived as 'successful'.

I feel the biggest trigger to action is awareness of your own mortality; you are not going to live for ever, and today, this month, this year, this downturn represents a significant chunk of your whole life.

Remember the exercise earlier in this book about which day of the week represents the decade you are: readers aged between 20 and 30 years old will be a Wednesday. I am a Saturday. There isn't much time to be a green shoot, and there is always a further uncertainty.

The one certain thing we have is that everything is uncertain. Two very different stories bring home how life is a gamble from the moment you wake up in the morning.

Britain's most unusual gravestone could well belong to Hannah Twynnoy a local barmaid in 18th century Wiltshire, whose grave lies at Malmesbury Abbey.

Little could she have known that she would lay claim to a dubious honour: the first person on record to be eaten by a tiger in Britain. Hannah apparently was thrilled at the arrival of a travelling circus, but ignored warnings against teasing the menagerie's tiger. It broke free and mauled her to death.

Or what about the story told by television reporter Alan Whicker in his autobiography, *'Whicker's War'* when he saw active service during World War II as a director of an army film crew with the British Eighth Army in Italy.

According to Whicker his commanding officer, Captain Sir Gerald Boles was 'allergic to lead', deeply anxious not be killed or injured. As a result he refused to go anywhere near the fighting, an evasiveness which infuriated the war correspondents under his care, and eventually led to him being transferred to a 'safer' posting away from the front.

Sadly for Sir Gerald, he was killed soon after his posting in a surprise Luftwaffe raid on the 'safe' port of Bari, when an ammunition ship harboured near his hotel took a direct hit.

These stories again highlight how life does not have its guarantees or certainties, and that you can never really be safe. Life is a terminal illness.

Your efforts to positively respond to the age of disruption - to become a green shoot and part of the Upturn - will be fuelled by putting it in a wider context of what you are doing with your life.

A further trigger for change, I would suggest, in addition to your sense of mortality, is your immortality. How are you going to be remembered after you have shaken off this mortal coil?

I remember a conversation I had while living in Yorkshire and driving my youngest daughter Lizzie, who was just four years old, and her friend Amber-Leigh. The topic was grandparents and I was explaining to her friend how Lizzie was just two weeks old when her grandfather died, so sadly, she never got to know him.

Amber-Leigh then added: *"My granddad died as well. But I always remember what he used to say to me."*

Touched by the comment, and intrigued by the prospect of finding out what this man's pearl of wisdom was to future generations, his legacy to his grandchildren, I asked: *"What did he used to say to you?"*

I was expectant, waiting for her to say something profound.

With absolutely no hint of irony or emotion Amber-Leigh passively replied: "He said '*Get out in ruddy garden!*'"

I could imagine the scene: a young child arrives at what I presume was an elderly, dour Yorkshireman's house. The young child is seen as a source of noise, inconvenience and disruption, and is being told, quite directly, to remove herself to the garden.

I was saddened for this child, that the one abiding memory of her grandfather was a negative one.

On further reflection I felt sadder for the grandfather; his sole legacy, family memory, would be as an unloving, disengaged, seemingly sour person, which I am sure, is not the complete picture.

He may well have been a wonderful human being, but his sticky phrase for future generations, his contribution to his folklore was five words: *"Get out in ruddy garden!"*

What's going to be your five word legacy? What are you going to do now, to be a green shoot for the Upturn, which in turn will be part of your wider life story?

Will your five words be:

'I WAS BEATEN BY DOWNTURN'
or
'UPTURN: I HELPED IT RISE'

It's your call. The second part of this book is yours to write.

To become a green shoot, and be a part of a wider Upturn please think flexibly, and think flexibly faster.

Now get growing.

The museum of Andy Green

All of us are living, breathing museums. Here is a map of my museum.

Gallery Level 1	Flexible and creative thinking skills	Communications: Propaganda (PR), memes, Brands and Personal brandcasting
Gallery Level 2	East London childhood Yorkshire adulthood Wales second childhood	Values: I hate waste of: • resources • talent • potential • opportunities • ideas

Gallery Level 1
You will discover a passion for flexible and creative thinking skills. Evidenced in several books, and in my work as a creativity consultant.

My other wing of core work skill is in the area of propaganda (PR), memes, brand communications, and personal brandcasting.

The word 'propaganda' may upset some people in the public relations profession. But I define 'propaganda' as: 'What you call other people's PR'

Memes are the DNA lifeblood of communications. Widely understood and used in scientific circles, less so in the communications industries, which is somewhat ironic.

Brands I regard as fundamental vehicles for how we communicate and how we can understand the world at large. Each of us is a brand.

Personal brandcasting is a term I coined in one of my books, to explain how great communicators come in all shapes and sizes but all do four key things: have strong personal brands (defined by icons, values and sexy facts); communicate through every dimension, where actions are more important than words; create effective memes, or word of mouth; network to build powerful personal networks

Gallery Level 2
My life experiences largely gathered in three locations. Born and brought up in the East End of London, one of five boys, my younger brother, Kevin, being profoundly autistic.

I have spent most of my adult life living, developing my professional skills and helping to bring up a family in Yorkshire, Recently, I have started a new home with my wife on beautiful Barry Island, experiencing what I call a 'second childhood'.

Our values drive our behaviours. My lead value is I hate waste, whether it is the planet's precious resources or individuals wasting their talent and potential, or opportunities and ideas being unfulfilled. (I recommend identifying your own core five values.)

What's your museum like?

Always say 'Thank You'

No matter how talented or brilliant you are, you will never achieve anything, or reach your full potential without the intervention, guidance or support of good, kind people.

Apologies for anyone not listed here who should be.

Thanks must go to:

Richard Jones and Nick Law at Tangent Books for their patience and kind support.

Dave Rattray for being the genius he is (and coming up with the cover design) and his support for the Flexible Thinking Forum.

My team of beta readers for being constructive friends, Anne Akers, Jackie Le Fevre, Alan Preece, Geoff Roberts, Bernard Savage and Heather Yaxley.

My career mentors, Steve McDermott for invaluable help, Barry Sheerman MP for being a good guy, David Taylor (the other one) and all the people whose sharing of their knowledge has helped me expand mine. Also, to Paul McGee, for the initial idea about the 1-10 scale for worse things to happen to you.

My connectors for making things happen for me.

The team and clients at GREEN communications, for putting up with me.

Nia Lynn Jones at Momentwm Public Relations for making my tour of Wales happen, and all the great local champions for doing their bit to help me, literally road test the material in this book in 15 events in four days (June 28th - July 3rd 2009).

Gareth Bickerton at UnLtd. for breaking the mould by not being a bureaucrat and for proving that an organization which promotes creativity, can actually be creative . Check them out at www.unltd.org.uk

My wife Judith, for putting up with my optimism, as well as for additional copy-editing and proof reading.

My brothers, Johnny, Micky, Peter, and especially Kevin.

My lovely daughters Charlotte and Lizzie for being who they are.

List of 5 things

People can generally only remember five things. Here are some lists to help you in becoming a green shoot and contribute to the wider Upturn.

5 key points from this book

1. Each of us is a green shoot – if you don't want to be a passive victim of the downturn, take responsibility and action, now!
2. Seeds of green shoots don't make news – prepare to be lonely, unloved, and laughed at. One day you will have lots of friends, be loved and admired, and you will laugh at the things they said could not be done. Also, the phrase 'green shoots' is taboo.
3. You're never alone however. Remember, your ancestors survived the Black Death – whatever is thrown at you doesn't compare with what your ancestors faced – do them proud.
4. Your flexibility driven by your flexible and creative thinking is the key to your resourcefulness. Creativity is flexible thinking around beautiful questions in your quest to add value
5. The tough don't just get going, they get going faster. You have to not just think flexibly. You have to think flexibly faster.

5 role models

1. The lieutenant character in the film *'Saving Private Ryan'* for being practical, resourceful and always doing the right thing.
2. The *'Rocky'* or *'Shawshank Redemption'* film characters for being ready to fight, and pick themselves up again and again.
3. Your mother, for always being there for you.
4. Barack Obama for being an inspirational example of achievement, but don't rely on him to save you.
5. Andy Green's brother Kevin. There is always someone else in this world who can make you count your blessings.

5 books to read

'The Creative Habit' by Twyla Tharp
'How to be a complete and utter failure' by Steve McDermott
'Authentic Happiness' by Martin E. Seligman
'How to be an Explorer of the World' by Keri Smith or *'Understanding Comics'* by Scott McCloud.
Any Classical literature you would not normally read.

5 Beautiful Questions

1. What is my beautiful question – what assumptions am I making?
2. How do I 'Big/Small/Different Box this?
3. What Red/ Green Light Thinking do I need to do?
4. How do I make this important/urgent/small step/ low risk/quick win?
5. What is my beautiful question – what assumptions am I now making?

Some things for you to make a list of

My 5 values
1.
2.
3.
4.
5.

My 5 role models
1.
2.
3.
4.
5.

The 5 things I am going to do today to become a green shoot
1.
2.
3.
4.
5.

The 5 things I am going to do by next month
1.
2.
3.
4.
5.

The 5 things I am going to do by next year
1.
2.
3.
4.
5.

The 5 things I am going to do before I kick the bucket
1.
2.
3.
4.
5.

The 5 words my descendants are going to tell their children about me:

-----------   -----------   -----------   -----------   -----------

Your daily flexibility diet

Sleep	Sleep somewhere different to the usual place, bed, side of bed...
Wake up	Use a different alarm, time, way of waking up, or stay in bed. Could you remove any clock from where you are sleeping?
Wake up routine	Always remember to capture your illuminations – the ideas which come out of the blue - particularly after incubation while you are asleep. What different ways can you capture these illuminations? Vary your routine of washing, eating, dressing.
Food	Try something new or different. (For example, try a piece of toast without the crust, or toasted just one side, with no butter or margarine – anything out of the ordinary.)
Travel	A friend complained how he found it depressing seeing the same people, waiting at the same time and places on the platform – go at a different, time, route, mode of transport was my suggestion. Can you vary your routine?

Encounters	When someone asks you: 'Are you alright? (or 'Awright'?) actually provide an answer, and share what's good about the day. Have a conversation with someone you wouldn't normally chat with. Find out about your taxi driver's life. Try a different newspaper, radio station, TV show
Incorporate Daily Surprises	See the suggestion of a menu on the next page. You can always flexibly add to it!
General	Go without e mail, your mobile phone, wearing your watch, jewellery, shoes for the day.
Daily retirement	Vary your time and routine, explore different ways you can finish the day on a positive note.

Your daily menu of surprises for your flexible life

People	Out of the blue contact someone you know. Get to know someone better. Make new friends. Discover a new person in your life today.
Place	Go somewhere different. Sit, sleep or go to a different toilet from your normal routine. Move something to an unfamiliar position.
Price	Go budget – find a new way of doing something cheaper or faster. Save money in some way. Go luxury – enjoy an indulgence. It can be small or something more extravagant. (Remember you only live once, and you can't take it with you.)
Product	Try something new Recycle or put something positive back into the environment. Do a different physical activity.
Promotion	Go out of your way to thank, or make known your appreciation of something you think is good, are thankful for, or would like to see more of.

Check out *your* Flexibility Quotient

Try a simple, easy-to-complete on-line test to measure you Flexibility Quotient by visiting:

www.flexiblethinking

The Flexible Thinking Forum is a not for profit social enterprise. It enables businesses and organizations to improve their people's creative thinking skills through conference speaking, training courses, training materials and facilitating organization awaydays.

The Forum aims to promote understanding and use of flexible and creative thinking among managers and decision-makers to overcome lazy or stupid thinking, improve performance, help people achieve more with less - and make the world a better place by doing so.

The Forum also assists third sector and other social enterprises with special services and subsidised activities generated from its profits.

Find out more - and check your Flexibility Quotient – by visiting the Forum's web site.

Other web sites for Andy Green include:

www.creativityatwork.co.uk

www.greencomms.com

www.twixtmas.co.uk

www.beatbluemonday.org.uk

Also by the author

'Overcoming Stupidity'

Is the world getting more stupid?

This book is written for anyone who feels that there is too much stupidity around us. It also explains why, in spite of massive technological advances to make us 'smarter', the opposite seems to happen.

Stupidity is not about low intelligence: we all know clever people who do stupid things. Rather it is caused by inflexible thinking without asking questions.

While there are many books highlighting the absurdities of modern life, this is perhaps a first to provide practical help. The book is a call to arms to use its inspiration, tools and ideas to fight back, combat, or least not feel so helpless when confronted with stupidity, whether it is dealing with bureaucrats, your boss, or for when the buck stops with you, this book will help.

Available, price £7, from Tangent Books
www.tangentbooks.co.uk

Other titles by Andy Green:
'Creativity in Public Relations' Kogan Page
'Effective Personal Communications' Kogan Page
'A Minute with Tony Blair' Pontefract Press